American Chick in Saudi Arabia

a memoir

Jean Sasson

Jacket design by www.HotDamnDesigns.com
Book design by Judith Engracia

For additional information about Jean Sasson and her books, please visit http://www.JeanSasson.com
Blog: http://jeansasson.wordpress.com/
Facebook: http://www.facebook.com/AuthorJeanSasson
Twitter: http://twitter.com/jeansasson

Other Works by Jean Sasson

Nonfiction:

The Rape of Kuwait

Princess: A True Story of Life Behind the Veil in Saudi Arabia

Princess Sultana's Daughters

Princess Sultana's Circle

Mayada, Daughter of Iraq

Love in a Torn Land: A Kurdish Woman's Story

Growing Up Bin Laden: Osama's Wife and Son Reveal their Secret World

For the Love of a Son: One Afghan Woman's Quest for her Stolen Child

Historical Fiction:

Ester's Child

Table of Contents

Introduction

Over the years, readers have asked me to share the stories of my personal adventures in the Middle East. I lived in Riyadh, Saudi Arabia, for an exciting twelve years, and I traveled throughout the Middle East for a total of thirty years. Several times I had begun writing my life story, but each time I got started, my phone would ring or an unexpected e-mail would drop into my in-box, and I would once again find myself pulled away from my own story and immersed in another's.

Whenever Princess Sultana or Mayada or Joanna or Omar and Najwa or Maryam offered me the opportunity to write about their amazing lives, I recognized that the world needed to hear their voices. Some of the courageous people whose stories I shared quite literally put their lives on the line, many of them risking torture, imprisonment, and unbearable tragedies— just to be heard. My own story seemed much less important in comparison.

But as change has once again roared across the Middle East, throwing once-stable societies into turmoil and revolution, thoughtful analysts have asked me to share my experiences. Journalists and academics and writers from many corners of the world have reached out to tap my personal knowledge, along with the glossaries and chronologies and maps that I've always included in the back of my books. That's when I remembered that I owned another treasure trove of history—of primary material—stored away in dusty boxes. I pulled open those old files and began to piece together my memories. Reminiscence drew me back in time to the many thrilling moments I had lived through while visiting these foreign lands. I had lived through so many exciting adventures that I soon realized that I was in danger of writing a two-thousand-page memoir. I decided instead to break my experiences into small pieces. In this new media world, publishing my adventures as stand-alones, as "shorts" or "singles," made perfect sense, at least as a beginning. Later I would pull together the most poignant stories into a traditionally published book.

And so I now return to the place where my own adventure began, to the Kingdom of Saudi Arabia.

As I gathered my thoughts, I couldn't stop looking at a smiling photograph of myself in 1978. A title for this "short" popped suddenly into consciousness. What a chick I was–in all senses of the word–how young and confident and innocent...just an American chick in Saudi Arabia.

In 1978, I was living in Jacksonville Beach, Florida, attending court reporting school. About nine months into the program, I reluctantly realized that life as a court reporter didn't suit my personality. Sitting in my seaside apartment on Jacksonville Beach one Sunday afternoon, I searched the newspaper employment ads, seeking a job that would give me time to discover what I really wanted to do. I had previously worked as the assistant for the administrator at a hospital in Alabama and I had loved my work there. While scanning the newspaper ads, my eye caught an intriguing post from Hospital Corporation of America, headquartered in Nashville, Tennessee. The recruiting agency sought a qualified person to take charge of organizing medical meetings at King Faisal Specialist Hospital & Research Centre (KFSH) in Riyadh, Saudi Arabia. My hospital experience in Alabama prepared me for the job. And, as a single woman without children, there was no reason I couldn't fly across the globe to assume the post. In fact, I quickly grew excited at the prospect of traveling thousands of miles so that I might experience a whole new country and an exotic new culture.

Six weeks later I was on my way to Nashville, where I was to undergo orientation before flying to London and then on to Riyadh. Although my parents and certain friends were nervous for me, I was so excited that I couldn't stop smiling. I loved my country, but I was ready to explore the world outside the United States.

Nineteen seventy-eight was a "happening" time in the region of the world in which I would be living, as one big news story after another made headlines. American president Jimmy Carter was working extremely hard with Egyptian president Anwar Sadat to strike a peace deal between Egypt and Israel. Just as I was leaving the United States, Carter, Sadat and Israeli president Menachim Begin gathered at Camp David, Maryland.

In Pakistan, Zulfikar Ali Bhutto was sentenced to death. In Lebanon, a United Nations force marched in to monitor Israel's "Operation Litani" invasion taking place in South Lebanon. In Iraq, Palestinian terrorist Wadia Haddad died under mysterious circumstances while under the dubious protection of Saddam Hussein. In Afghanistan, a revolution bubbled and boiled over, sated only when the president and his family were murdered. Jordan's King Hussein married American Lisa Halaby, who took the name of Queen Noor. And in two countries that directly bordered Saudi Arabia–Yemen and Southern Yemen–coups toppled the existing regimes.

Few places on earth could match the Muslim Middle East for political intrigue and economic excitement.

After an informative week of travel to Nashville and London, I arrived in the desert city of Riyadh, Saudi Arabia. From the first moment that my feet touched the soil of Riyadh, I was forever changed. I felt an instant and passionate connection to the country and to the people. I was never frightened or shy or nervous; I was instead intensely curious about the many lovely people I met, including hospital employees from three hundred different countries.

I lived with two other single women in the gated and guard-protected Medical City Village, with all the other single women working at the hospital. I was employed as the administrative secretary in charge of doctor's meetings. Less than two years later, I was promoted to Administrative Coordinator of Medical Affairs, working directly for the physician head of the hospital, a Saudi cardiologist named Nizar Feteih.

Within a month of arriving at the hospital, I was introduced to Peter Sasson. Peter's father was Jewish with an Italian and British family background. Peter's mother was Catholic Yugoslavian. Peter was a cosmopolitan man who was raised in the Church of England, spoke six languages fluently, and was a world traveler. He was also head of an insurance company operating in the kingdom. Peter was the only person I dated in the kingdom and we soon fell in love; four years later, we married.

Through Peter, who lived in a villa in a Saudi neighborhood and who was sponsored by a prominent Saudi family, and through Dr. Feteih, who enjoyed a close relationship with King Khalid and Crown Prince Fahd, I met Saudis from all social classes. I came to know Bedouins, city Saudis from the professional class, and a few members of the royal family. Through Dr. Feteih I even met King Khalid and Crown Prince Fahd, both of whom were very considerate and kind.

The Middle East was changing just as radically as I was. In 1979, events exploded in the Middle East and for the first time Americans became aware of the insecurity and religious divides that unsettle the region. Many people were shocked and dismayed by the fall of the Shah of Iran in January 1979 and by the subsequent expulsion of his family from their country. That troubling incident was followed by the violent Mecca uprising in November 1979. The episodes together rocked the Saudi government.

Since the kingdom was moving toward modernization, most Saudis and many Westerners believed that Saudi women would soon benefit from a loosening of rigid rules. But such was not to come, for the Saudi government was so wary of the religious clerics that they wanted to do nothing to turn the powerful religious establishment against the regime. Little did I foresee that one day I would become involved with one of the few Saudi women willing to put herself at risk to bring change to Saudi females.

But I'm getting ahead of myself. First let me take you back with me to the year 1978, and give you a brief peek into the beginning of my adventure in the desert kingdom.

Chapter One
Touchdown in a Magical Kingdom

In my childhood fantasies, a kingdom was always a magical place. So when I first enter a faraway land ruled by kings, the moment feels surreal. I first arrive in the desert city of Riyadh on September 7, 1978. I have flown in on a fully booked Saudia jumbo jet from London. Once the aircraft lands and the doors open, hot air gushes into the airplane. I grimace with shock.

Soon after landing, passengers are loaded into a crammed bus to be taken to the airport terminal. There is nowhere for us to sit on the bus because all available seats are already occupied by Saudi men. Even pregnant or elderly Arab women are standing. As the bus begins to move, we strap-clutching women and children sway and collide with the erratic movements of the vehicle, while only men sit in comfort, staring stoically out the bus windows.

I nearly lose my balance as passengers roughly push to get off the bus. I am pushed along in the crowd and through the terminal door. The airport swarms with people moving in many directions. Suddenly a burst of unintelligible voices greets me; the noise and the chaos feels like a human assault. I stand motionless until someone behind gives me a not-so-gentle push into a long line of people waiting to get their passports stamped to gain entry into the kingdom.

Foreign visitors find obtaining permission to enter the closed society of Saudi Arabia is enormously complicated. This is not a country that allows tourists. Only those foreigners needed to work in hospitals, schools, construction, or in the oil business are allowed entry. The rulers of the kingdom fairly recently resolved to leap across centuries of primitive life and bound into the modern world. Thus, they reluctantly opened the doors to welcome a host of foreign workers. Thankfully, everything about my visit was handled by Hospital Corporation of America (HCA), so no problems are expected.

The meandering human lines barely move as dour-faced Saudi officials stamp innumerable pages in an endless chain of passports. I repeatedly check the documents I hold in my hands, and when I finally pass them to the Saudi bureaucrat, I stare at him as he stares at me. He is tall and slim with a youthful face, albeit a face with a serious expression. But after shifting his gaze from my face to my passport photo, he surprises me with an open sweet smile, and says, "Welcome. Welcome to the Kingdom of Saudi Arabia."

Relieved and happy to be pleasantly greeted, I smile back before joining yet another long line. Our suitcases must be searched.

Everything in this new world is so different from anything I have ever known. I steal looks at the Saudi men. Most are tall and slim, the same as the young man who stamped my passport. All are wearing the same type of dress, a long white shirt that reaches to the ankles. This, I know, is called a *thobe*. The men also are wearing similar head gear, a red-and-white–checkered cloth known as the *shamagh*. This headdress is held in place by a black band called an *agal*. I can easily understand how their white dress and head covering is the best costume to wear in the desert. Considering the heat, I have a fleeting idea that I might wear one of those dresses myself. I wonder if there is a penalty for women wearing men's clothing.

The women's black cloaks and veils are another matter. I can only imagine how hot and uncomfortable such an outfit must be in the Saudi sun.

Looking from the men to the women, I recall the warnings of well-meaning friends who advised me *not* to travel to a country where personal freedoms for women are so limited. Concerned friends also raised questions about living in a country ruled by a monarchy, a regime whose authority is built on the back of the warlike Wahhabi sect of Islam. But I dismissed their concerns. I was born with a bold spirit and harbor no fear of new horizons.

The line inches closer to the serious-faced men who will inspect my bags. Alcohol, pork, and pornography are strictly forbidden in the kingdom. But after growing up in a tiny Southern town in America's "Bible Belt," I am accustomed to a conservative lifestyle. Going without these three items will pose no hardship for me. As the daughter of an alcoholic, I've never tasted alcohol. I've seen pornography only once, and that was by accident. And pork is a food I can readily forego. But Saudi law censors other, "harmless" items that spur my concern. Books by Jewish authors, such as Herman Wouk and Leon Uris–two favorite writers–are forbidden. Christian crosses, the Holy Bible, and even women's magazines are banned. I'm an avid reader and have packed many books and magazines. Might I inadvertently have committed a crime?

The screech of a child grabs my attention. I observe a black-cloaked woman who stands obediently behind her Saudi man, an infant crying in her arms while two toddlers clutch at her long black cloak. That woman's life is so unlike my own that we might as well be from different planets. I am a single female traveling around the world to live alone in a country where I do not know anyone. She is a woman who most likely married early to a man she met for the first time on her wedding day. Like most Saudi women, every decision that affects her life is made by a man.

Perhaps Saudi men wish to keep their females forever children?

My attention moves to settle on a second Saudi family. A lone man is trailed by six veiled women who are tasked with mothering nine or ten small children. Since Islamic law limits Muslim men to four wives, I suppose that several of the women are his wives while the remainder of the shrouded figures could be daughters who have reached the age where they must be fully covered.

For a weird, brief moment, I feel an unexpected emotion. I would love to be on the other side of that restrictive veil, to know exactly what it feels like to be shrouded in black. Otherwise, I'll never understand the limits of their lives. I watch in fascination as the no-faced women begin to cheep and titter under their veils. Numerous children are shoving and shouting, harassing their mothers with the boundless energy of youth.

The dominating husband is obviously exhausted by the work of attending to such a large group of women and children.

I study his face carefully, realizing that I had noticed this same man's flurry of activity while I gathered my own luggage. He had rushed to collect his family's many suitcases. Now, with hurried movements, he lined the colorful bags in a perfect file. Then he did the same for his wives, first gesturing at the cases and then at the women, shouting at one veiled woman after another until his brown face darkened with pique. I assume from the reactions of the veiled women that each one was put in charge of an individual suitcase, since now each woman stands tranquil beside an overstuffed case. I feel disloyal to my sex when I smile, thinking how the women resemble a row of watchful black birds on a wire. Shifting my gaze to the man once again, I smile even wider. This greedy man has overburdened himself by taking so many women as wives. I chuckle. It serves him right.

Chapter Two
Checking into the Desert Kingdom

As I wait, I carefully examine the flat tables of the customs officials, tables that creak beneath the weight of enormous suitcases stuffed with innumerable goods from every part of the world. People ahead of me appear increasingly nervous. Their apprehension seems to heighten as they approach the dreaded Saudi officials who eagerly search for contraband in luggage. The Saudi officials appear to grow more and more enthusiastic, suspiciously examining each item of clothing or personal article in the full-to-bursting cases.

I'm not looking forward to the scrutiny of the customs officials. When I see an official hold up a magazine and shout angrily at a young European man, my anxiety grows.

I mutter louder than I intend. "Good Lord! What a mess!"

A man from England is standing a few inches to my right. He turns to face me. "Your first time to the kingdom?" he inquires with a genial expression.

With a grimace, I nod. "Yes." I add, "This is my first time in the Middle East, actually."

He grins broadly. "There are very few Western women living in Riyadh. And single females are as rare as flawless diamonds, and are treated as such. You will have an easy go of it, believe me."

I nod in understanding. I had been warned by the recruiters at HCA. In 1978, there are few foreign women living in the kingdom, although there are many foreign men. I'm betting that most single females receive more attention than they want. Although I am single and will most likely meet and date someone while living in the kingdom, meeting men was not my purpose for traveling to Saudi Arabia. I'm in it for the adventure and travel and getting to personally observe a part of the world I know so little about.

My gaze returns to the women covered in black cloaks. What dreams do these women have? Do they dream of tossing those veils in the trash? Do they dream of telling their bossy husband to take a hike? Do they dream of education, or a career? Do they dream at all, or do they calmly accept that they live in a world in which men not only make all the rules, but also enforce them.

Soon I am standing in front of a man who is handling my personal items. For a moment he is stern, but soon he is chatting cordially, asking questions about my background. He surprises me when he asks, "Do you look like your mother? Do you look like your father?" He listens intently as though I am giving him American state secrets when I tell him, "Neither really, although I have my mother's blonde hair and light eyes."

"That's good," he says with a big smile. "Your father is lucky to have a blonde wife." His eyes sparkle in friendliness. "He is the father of a beautiful blonde daughter, too."

His conversation takes his attention away from his job and he fails to properly search my bags. In fact, four of my eight bags remain closed for inspection. I am taken aback when he questions me on personal matters, such as where I will work and if I have a boyfriend.

The moment grows awkward for me, but the official is happily chatting and doesn't seem to notice that I do not respond to many questions.

Finally, with a friendly wave he wishes me off, "Have a good time in my country." His smile grows wider. "Perhaps I will see you when you travel again?"

I don't respond. I hear my name called and look to see that my travel companions are gathering at the departure area. I point them out to the Yemeni baggage worker as I rush to join my group. We have been met by a cheerful Egyptian named Mousa. Mousa is a giant of a man with a broad smile. He proudly relates that he is the head of the King Faisal Travel Department. Mousa guides us to a bus that has been provided by the hospital.

It's late in the evening and I'm relieved that the drive across the busy city takes less than thirty minutes. I shift my thoughts to consider where I am going to spend most of my life over the next two years. The King Faisal Medical City is in reality a small but self-sufficient city inside the bustling municipality of Riyadh. The hospital is said to be one of the world's most up-to date centers of medical science and technology. The Medical City complex consists of the hospital, residential and recreational areas for the hospital staff, and an engineering services complex consisting of electrical, water, sewer and air-conditioning plants.

We soon arrive, but I am so tired that I notice very little.

When housing units are assigned I learn that I'll live in a three-bedroom apartment in Medical City Village (MCV) with two other unmarried women who have been hired to work at the medical institution. Joy is an attractive blonde American woman who is a skilled medical technician in radiology. Jenny is a nurse, a dark-skinned, beautiful woman originally from Sri Lanka who holds a British passport.

The accommodations are plain but adequate. The unit has a basic kitchen, combined living and dining room, three bedrooms, and one full bath and a half bath. This will do, I tell myself, as I make a grateful mental note that both roommates appear cordial. Despite the necessity to co-exist in small quarters, I believe that we will get along easily. I'm even more optimistic when I learn that both Joy and Jenny are also non-smokers.

We all rush to disappear behind closed doors into our individual bedrooms. My mind is still racing but I force myself to close my eyes and summon sleep.

Chapter Three
Allah Akbar

I am abruptly awakened by the sound of a loud but sonorous male voice. *"Allah Akbar! Allah Akbar! Allah Akbar!"* I rub my eyes. Why is a man wailing?

Then I know that I am hearing a *muezzin*, the Muslim cleric assigned the job of calling the faithful to pray. Evidently there is a mosque very near our apartment building. It is sunrise and time for the first prayer of the day. We have been told that the Saudi government builds mosques in every neighborhood in the kingdom so that the faithful can walk to prayer. With five prayers each day, I can understand the need.

Enormously enchanted by the *muezzin's* haunting cry, I instinctively know then that I have made the right decision to accept a job in a foreign land. Any previous doubts are pushed aside at leaving my small-town life to travel around the world and live in a land ruled by kings.

I continue to listen to the call to pray, a prayer that is repeated in hundreds of thousands of mosques all over the world:

> *Allah Akbar!* (God is most great!) *Allah Akbar!*
> *Allah Akbar!*
> I bear witness that there is no God but Allah. I bear
> witness that
> there is no God but Allah. I bear witness that there
> is no God but Allah.
> I bear witness that Muhammed is the Apostle of
> Allah! I bear witness that

Muhammed is the Apostle of Allah! I bear witness
        that Muhammed is the Apostle of Allah!
Come to prayer! Come to prayer! Come to prayer!
Come to success! Come to success! Come to
        success!
Allah Akbar! Allah Akbar! Allah Akbar!
There is no God but Allah!

It feels magical to me to know that five times each day, nearly a billion believing Muslims are reciting the same prayer and are synchronized in the same postures, all across the slow-turning earth.

I return to bed and fall asleep. A few hours later, my excitement overcomes my fatigue when I rush from the apartment to join the other new hires that traveled with me from Nashville and London. We are to be taken via bus on a short tour of the desert city.

First we take a quick drive past the hospital[1], the place I will spend six out of seven days a week. The hospital is built of unusual tawny-shaded stones that have been perfectly fitted to form the exterior wall, giving it a golden hue. A circular driveway takes us past a decorative water fountain. The hospital is surrounded by carefully tended grounds carpeted with immense beds of green bushes and vividly colored flowers, something I did not expect in the middle of a desert.

We leave the vast hospital complex and travel Riyadh's main streets, which are modern boulevards. Enormous construction projects are ongoing and fill the skyline with hundreds of gigantic building cranes. The sight of endless building cranes causes a lot of talk in the bus. The shiny exteriors of modern skyscrapers mirror neighboring mud dwellings. Riyadh is nothing like I had expected.

---

[1] For photos of The King Faisal Hospital and Research Center, please visit http://jeansasson.com/books/american-chick-gallery.html

The name Riyadh is the plural of *rowdhah*, an Arabic word which means an area where grass can be found for grazing camels or sheep. To simplify matters, the city became commonly known as "the gardens." Riyadh was part of a series of villages along the Wadi Hanifa. Although surrounded by sand on three sides, it grew into a walled city and a trading post on the historic route to Mecca.

During the drive to the downtown area, our guide provides us with additional facts and figures about the country, the citizens, and about proper Muslim etiquettes.

The monotone of our guide's voice is difficult to follow from my seat near the back of the bus. Her words fade and my attention drifts, my curiosity occasionally piqued by intriguing scenes along the city streets.

White-*thobed* men are sauntering up and down the sidewalks. Many of the men are paired and walk hand-in-hand. I know from my reading that such intimacy between men is not uncommon in this part of the world and signifies only friendship without any sexual component.

There is only a smattering of veiled women present. I search, but I cannot find a single uncovered Arab female face.

Some women are sitting on the sidewalks, staring at a passing world through the black gauze of their veils. For a Westerner unaccustomed to Saudi customs, the image of veiled Saudi women proves addictive. I really cannot stop staring at female forms covered in black gauze and long cloaks sweeping the streets.

We soon arrive at Dira Square[2], where the famous clock tower comes into view. This square has been nicknamed "Chop-Chop Square" by foreigners. I'm told that I'm looking at a macabre place where the kingdom's

---

[2] For a photo of Dira Square, please visit
http://jeansasson.com/books/american-chick-gallery.html

criminals lose hands, feet, and heads. I find it ironic that the Palace of Justice sits on the square. Saudi Arabia is a country that places the welfare of the society above the welfare of the individual. Crime rates are low and government officials attribute their country's enviable crime statistics to the swift punishment doled out to criminals.

When our guide points out the Musmak Fortress, a dried mud citadel in the center of old Riyadh, my imagination soars, taking me back to the dramatic saga that imbued the dynasty of the al Saud family. I know from my reading that during the raid, a spear was heaved so forcefully that nearly one hundred years later that ancient weapon is still lodged in the doorway. I feel the enthusiasm of a child, wanting to see that spear for myself.

Although the kingdom has benefited by its unification, in many ways the citizens of the kingdom have paid dearly for the victory of the al-Saud, the family that pulled the country together and which still rules it. To succeed with his plans to conquer all of Arabia, founder Abdul Aziz enlisted the religious zealots to his cause, creating a special unit of religious police.

That first-formed unit of fanatics grew into what is now known as the religious police, the *Mutawain*, austere men with an abominable record of human misery trailing their *thobes*.

The king and his Wahhabi followers condemned everything they did not understand. Under Abdul Aziz, the harshest interpretations of the Koran became law. Applying the most severe tenets of Islam, these ignorant men even dismantled a highly developed legal system in the Hejaz and shut down the civil courts.

There were many bloody episodes when this band of cruel Wahhabi defended the faith with the sword, plunging it into the unbeliever's belly as far as possible.

Envisioning the violence of sharp swords meeting human flesh, I jump in surprise when someone touches my shoulder and says, "Jean. Let's go."

We disembark the bus to stroll through the old shopping bazaar.

Perhaps I'll see one of the religious police, the *Mutawain*. I've been told that the merciless men can be recognized by their henna-dyed beards and their ankle-length *thobes*. I'm also warned that many of the men carry a camel whip or a thick stick to beat people. These are the men who have been appointed responsible for the morals of all people residing in the kingdom, including foreign workers.

I will be on the lookout.

But all thoughts of mean-tempered religious police quickly diminish in the face of the colorful human drama that unfolds before my eyes. A welter of cries in many tongues encharges this new environment.

Unsmiling money changers lounge behind small wooden desks, quietly tidying mounds of international currencies scattered in jumbled piles.

The aroma of the spice souk drifts out of an alleyway, overwhelming my nostrils with unfamiliar pungent odors. A woman in our party generates enthusiasm after purchasing a tiny bag of frankincense.

Multicolored Damascus silks swing from the ceiling, swaying in a light breeze side by side with the black cloaks and veils worn by Saudi women.

Bedouin daggers, tarnished spears, and antique firearms hang along walls. Brightly colored and authentic camel bags conceal silver-decorated wooden chests. Wooden camel milk bowls lie in disorderly piles.

The carpet souk brings to mind ancient tales from *The Arabian Nights*. In one open stall, a mountain of rolled carpets lies stacked in dusty neglect while the raffish owner sits cross-legged in a corner, his darting eyes filled with cunning, scrutinizing the crowd for sign of a potential client.

We have been forewarned by our guide that we are expected to enter into a lively bargaining process with shopkeepers for any item in the souks.

Our fascinating but brief introduction to the merchant sector of the city ends quickly when our guide says it is time to return to the bus.

I depart without complaint, knowing that I will have at least two years to explore this land, the customs, and the inhabitants.

Chapter Four
A Hospital Fit for a King

Soon we arrive at the hospital, large glass doors slide silently open as we eagerly push, wide-eyed, through the front entrance to behold the most beautiful hospital in the kingdom, maybe in the world. The finest materials were used; deep plush carpets make you feel that you are walking on air and it's rumored that gold was used in vast quantities through the entire building.

After leaving college, I worked for six years in a hospital in the United States; the hustle and bustle of this royal hospital feels comforting and familiar.

Many Saudi male visitors to the hospital walk through the lobby[3] wearing bewildered expressions, searching for the correct department. A few men are trailed by three or four women. The women's expressions are unknown because they are all veiled.

All patients were Saudi in national dress, only the occasional staff member clothed in hospital uniform or western dress broke the kaleidoscope of men in brilliant white starched *thobes* with red-and-white-checkered *shamaghs*; the women concealed head to foot in black *abaaya*s appeared like black specters moving respectfully behind their men, their masters.

The King Faisal Hospital and Research Centre is a specialist hospital built especially by Saudi Arabia's third king, King Faisal, to supplement the care provided by existing general hospitals within the kingdom. Other than

---

[3] For a photo of the lobby of the hospital, please visit
http://jeansasson.com/books/american-chick-gallery.html

certain members of the royal family, and employees of the hospital, every patient admitted into the hospital has been referred from another institution or from a high-ranking member of the royal family. The hospital only has two hundred and fifty admitting beds, so medical admissions are at a premium and greatly coveted by all Saudis.

The extended corridor of the hospital seems a mile long, diverging into areas reserved for administration, specialty medical clinics, private patients' rooms, rehabilitation services, dining facilities, and a pharmacy. Because of the large expatriate community, there's a multitude of conveniences for employees, including recreation areas and even a bank. Before oil money flowed freely, there were few doctors or medical clinics in the kingdom. The ill and dying had little hope of receiving up-to-date medical treatment. Popular treatments were often barbaric.

A cancerous tumor might be removed with a dagger.

Abdominal discomfort was treated by drinking the urine of a camel.

If pain became intense, cautery was the only treatment. Bottles or daggers were held over open flames then held against the parts of the body traditional Bedouin doctors' regarded as appropriate for the illness they were treating. Even tiny infants and young children were cauterized.

Ruling a land where a simple flesh wound could deliver a slow and agonizing death, King Faisal dreamed of building the finest medical facility in the world. He wanted every Saudi, rich or poor, to have access to the most advanced medical care possible.

As early as 1965, Faisal donated one million square meters of his own land for the hospital site. Although a thrifty man, no expense was spared for his favorite project. Technology from around the world was imported to build, equip, and staff the sophisticated hospital.

28

As we walk through the luxurious hospital lobby to those sliding doors, suddenly I am within inches of King Faisal ibn Abdul Aziz al-Saud's face. I stand silently and stare at the official royal portrait of King Faisal. The illuminated portrait in mosaic consisting of lapis-lazuli and other semi-precious stones hang in the already imposing hospital entrance. Faisal, the third king of Saudi Arabia was a somber-faced man. Bushy black brows dominate his deeply lined brow. Heavy lids droop over large brown eyes that appear resolute yet are glazed with a sad weariness. His aggressive nose angles over a gray speckled mustache and goatee. An unmistakable stoicism lines his face, revealing a lifetime accumulation of disillusionments. His hands held before his face in constant prayer silently speak of his devotion to his God and to his people.

Many believe that under King Faisal's watchful eye, Saudi Arabia was more wisely governed than any other time in the kingdom's history. In his determination to pull Saudi Arabia into the modern world, he made thousands of enemies and an equal number of friends. In one of the bitterest moments in modern Arabian history, this dedicated man was shot to death by one of his nephews. Murdered only three years before, shortly before the grand opening of the medical facility, King Faisal never saw the exciting result of his dream.

A gentle hand is laid on my shoulder. "Jean, it's time to visit a few more departments now." I turn to see a friendly smile freely given from one of my new acquaintances.

Walking past the admitting office, I am a witness to a heartbreaking scene. A young Bedouin girl, who looks to be ten or eleven years old, is squirming while sitting in a wheelchair. The child is in obvious pain. I quickly ascertain that she is an incoming patient waiting to be admitted into the hospital.

She lifts her head.

I gasp and fling one hand over my mouth. Before my eyes is a human nightmare. The child's face is hideous. A grisly mass of blue-and red-tinged flesh covers one eye, her nose, and even edges into her mouth! How is it possible for this child to eat any solid food? I notice that her lips move slightly and silently as though she is praying.

A Bedouin man wearing a soiled *thobe* stands beside her. A veiled woman stands to the side.

Suddenly the girl's unaffected eye meets my dismayed gaze.

Caught with my expression of horror, I'm acutely embarrassed, yet I can't pull my attention away from this young girl.

I overhear a doctor speaking in English to a translator. "Tell her parents that their daughter's surgery is scheduled for tomorrow. I believe her tumor is non-malignant. After we remove the tumor, she will be scheduled for plastic surgery to repair the damage." He kindly comforts the father with the good news, "She will soon return with you to your village and resume a normal life."

The Bedouin gives a brave grimace as he nods in understanding.

How lovely that all people have dreams. I tremble to think of that girl's slow and agonizing death if not for the dream of a king. I quickly walk away, my mood as joyful as if I have won a grand prize to be a small part of this medical institution.

Chapter Five
Medical Affairs

After a busy day, I return to our apartment and begin unpacking my belongings. The days that follow pass quickly, and I settle into my new environment with ease; my home life is comfortable and my work is challenging.

In Medical Affairs, I work closely with Rosalyn, a very attractive American woman from Pennsylvania who has been at the hospital for more than a year. Rosalyn has a gracious personality, and she generously takes the time to lead me through the complications of expatriate life.

I had been told by HCA of Nashville that dating was not allowed in the kingdom, but I really could not believe that would be the case. From the beginning of time, unattached males and females always find ways to link up. It quickly becomes clear that I was right. Living in a land where the native female population is veiled and kept out of public life, every unattached, expatriate woman at the hospital has many social invitations every day from European and American men, and not least from Arab men. My experience in this matter was no exception. From the first moment I arrive in Riyadh, I'm inundated with social invitations. As an unattached woman, I have the opportunity to date many single men.

I refuse most social invitations because I'm in no rush to involve myself in a rash of engagements. Everyday life in the kingdom is busy with work and with new friends.

Despite my happy single state, Rosalyn soon connects me to a European man she knows and whom she wants me to meet. The man's name is Peter Sasson. "Peter is an international man," Rosalyn tells me. "He is a European born in Egypt and raised in Great Britain." She adds, "He's good looking and very likable." She smiles widely when she adds, "Peter is one of the most entertaining people I have met since coming to Riyadh."

Trusting Rosalyn's judgment, I soon accept a telephone call from Peter Sasson and agree to a first date. I've never been on a blind date in my life, but when the doorbell rings at my apartment in MCV, I open the door and my sense of unease vanishes.

Peter Sasson[4] is not tall, but he has a good height. He has the form of an athlete with broad shoulders and a slim body. His dark brown hair is striking but carelessly groomed. He has deep-set, penetrating brown eyes. He has a distinguished nose and full lips. His skin is olive.

Although Peter Sasson is delightfully handsome, I'm most pleased to see that this man is marked by an easy-going nature. His ready smile is bright and amiable. I *like* sunny personalities, and when he speaks, his charming British lilt adds the perfect touch.

By the end of the evening, I sense that Peter Sasson will stamp his strong personality on my Saudi experience. After we make plans for a second date, we say goodnight at the door of my apartment.

I go to sleep enthusiastic and happy that I accepted the challenge to travel around the world. I hope my modest skills will help to support this newly formed hospital, and during my stay that I will have the opportunity to travel to many foreign countries.

Something tells me that I've made the best decision of my life. I fall asleep awaiting the sounds of the morning call to prayer, *Allah Akbar...Allah Akbar...*drifting through the air.

---

[4] For a photo of Peter Sasson, please visit
http://jeansasson.com/books/american-chick-gallery.html

Chapter Six
Wearing the Veil

No one knows my dangerous secret. Although I've been a resident of the Kingdom of Saudi Arabia for less than a year, already I am involved in a risky adventure. I am swathed in the complete Saudi veil[5], walking through the aisles of the Dirrah gold souk during the mid-morning July heat of Riyadh. I easily find refuge in the anonymity of the crowd of black-cloaked women browsing the shopping bazaar, yet I am nothing like the veiled women surrounding me. Saudi shoppers on all sides of me are unaware that a blonde, fair-skinned American is walking among them, as one of them.

Generally I would be at my office on a Thursday morning. But I have taken the day off for a specific purpose, to discover more about the life of a Saudi woman.

Female life in Saudi Arabia is not perfect for any woman, not even for foreign women. In fact, there are many restrictions in place for expatriate women at the hospital, and these rules cover a wide range of behaviors, including a ban against dating Saudis or any Arab. There is an order to dress modestly, a ban upon driving an automobile, pedaling a bicycle, drinking alcohol, or becoming involved in social topics such as the issue of women's rights or in political topics such as the ruling family. Women's issues are the most taboo subject, and during orientation all employees were warned to stay

---

[5] For a photo of conservative Muslim attire, please visit
http://jeansasson.com/books/american-chick-gallery.html

away from the dangerous topic of discrimination against women.

I readily relinquished my right to drive and to bicycle, for Riyadh traffic is downright hazardous! I prefer being a passenger protected in the back seat. I always dress modestly, for I do respect the culture of the country that has so warmly welcomed me. I have never dated any Arab, for I understand the personal problems that would arise for a woman with my particular assertive personality. I never drink alcoholic beverages because I cannot even bear the odor of alcohol, and strongly dislike how most people misbehave after having a few drinks. Yet I cannot claim perfection in abiding by the rules, because I can scarcely restrain myself from speaking out about women's issues.

Since I was a teenager, the right of all women to live in dignity and to escape discrimination has been at the forefront of my personal goals. Even at an early age, I recognized the most common human conflict in the world: the power of men over women.

For a full year I have been biding my time and holding my tongue, saying and doing nothing as I observe the lives of Saudi women. Being young and blonde and considered attractive by many Saudis, I am treated like a princess nearly everywhere I go. Most native or Muslim women from other Arab countries are less fortunate. I have come to know many tragic stories.

As I assumed when I first arrived in the kingdom, all important hospital files cross our desks in Medical Affairs. We are notified when Saudi husbands divorce wives who are disease-stricken, or who abandon them in the hospital after the wife births too many daughters. We hear when Saudi female patients are beaten nearly to death by their husbands. It's not uncommon for a Saudi man to visit his disease-weakened wife and insist she sleep on the floor or in a chair while the husband spends the night in her bed.

Such stories are hard for a woman like me to hear. I admit that I can do nothing to assist any helpless women, for in Saudi Arabia, Saudi males are supreme and their superiority is supported by every government agency and religious authority.

Although I can never be a Saudi woman, and will never live the life of a Muslim woman in Saudi Arabia, the one thing I can do is don the face veil and walk the souks. Now I will know exactly how it feels to walk about without being seen, for the black face veil makes women invisible.

My good mood slowly changes. This is in part because of physical discomfort. My stroll has become physically laborious. The souk is not air-conditioned; the pathways are so narrow and so crowded that no breeze stirs. I flap my arms and open up the front of my cloak, drawing a few disapproving stares from the men around me. I shiver with annoyance at their disapproval.

Saudi females are forbidden nearly everything natural to ordinary modern life.

Most females are forced to veil.

Women are forbidden to drive.

Girls are forbidden to date and are obligated to agree to arranged marriages. Most worrisome, young girls can be given in marriage to men twice their age as the second, third, or fourth wife.

A first wife cannot prevent her husband from taking a second or third and even a fourth wife. Some women are unaware of their husband's additional marriage plans until he brings the new brides home.Women have no legal authority to block their husbands from acquiring concubines or traveling to sex-for-hire establishments in Asia.

Wives cannot stop their husbands from divorcing them, even if there is no good cause.

Women cannot protest if their fathers, husbands, brothers, or even sons confine them to their homes.

Females are limited to certain professions. They are not allowed to work with or near men who are not of their family.

Women are prohibited from managing most businesses.

Females are not permitted to eat in most restaurants, or even to enter many shops.

Females are forbidden from traveling unless they have written permission from a male family member.

Females in Saudi Arabia have so little authority and power over their own fate that it is wrenchingly painful to witness. From daughter, to sibling, to wife, to mother, the women of Arabia move through a lifelong loop of complete male domination.

The imposition of the full veil gives men the ultimate control instrument. The full face veil is not required by their God, so why should it be required by their families, their government, or religious clerics?

So long as the Saudi men are able to ensure their women are veiled from head to toe, there are few tasks that a Saudi woman can realistically accomplish.

I have been in the full veil for less than an hour and I can hardly walk while so ensnarled in the black garments. I can understand how the veil would prohibit a woman from assuming various jobs. To perform the responsibilities of my current job would be impossible. I have to be able to move rapidly, read and type quickly, and act on many documents, as well as perform many other mundane office tasks.

Several times I have asked modern-thinking Saudis, "What dark mind fashioned the black veils of Riyadh?"

No Saudi Arabian can give me a satisfactory answer. It seems impossible to follow the exact trail of the veiling custom. Although the veil is barely mentioned in the Koran, it *is* known that veiling can be traced from Persia, Turkey, and India, and that the custom was adopted by Arabia's nomadic tribes. Sadly, this ancient tradition survived into modern life. Even now, even in the twenty-first century, Saudi girls and women must cover their body, hair, and face.

I had worn the veil once before, but that event hardly mattered since it was for a frivolous purpose.

Several months after arriving in the kingdom, Dr. Whitehill, a dentist at the KFSH, assisted me in playing a harmless prank on some unsuspecting hospital friends.

Dr. Padmos and his wife, Pat, had invited me to a private dinner party. The party was planned during the Eid al-Adha Muslim feast. This feast comes at the end of the Haj pilgrimage, one of several occasions in Muslim countries when the wealthy share with the poor.

During this holiday time, veiled Saudi women loitered at the gates of Medical City Village, their palms outstretched. Although most of the women happily accepted the occasional small-denomination riyal note or halalah coin, a few veiled women aggressively voiced their displeasure with the limited charity sometimes handed out. There were rumors that several veiled women had even followed some expatriates into the village, screeching at them in angry Arabic.

The hostile veiled women made everyone in the village edgy.

Dr. Whitehill and I planned the prank very carefully around the theme of an impoverished and hungry veiled woman displeased with the charity extended to her.

On the evening appointed for my practical joke, I dressed carefully in my full Saudi veil, which I had purchased a few weeks after arriving in Riyadh. I then hid behind a large bush alongside the Padmos household. When the party was in full swing, Dr. Whitehill arrived and knocked on the front door. As Dr. Padmos opened the door to welcome his dentist friend, I moved quickly, jumping from behind the bush, lightly shoving the men aside to rush past them into the home.

I paused in the middle of the small sitting room, swiveling my head left and right, searching for the food.

While the men stood immobilized in disbelief, female revelers began to scream and retreat to the corners of the room. Everyone believed the party had been crashed by a crazed veiled woman.

But the fun had not yet ended. When I caught sight of the heavily laden table, I groaned hungrily two or three times and hurried past the women to the table. Guests began dropping their food to the floor and scrambling to avoid me while I shoved foodstuff into a large black bag I carried.

The high-pitched screeches of the expatriate women grew even louder. Amusing to me, none of the men took one step to stop me.

I hurried through the room with the precious food held to my chest. At the doorway, I turned, yanked the veil from my face, and shouted, "Prank!"

That evening was enormous fun. And the entertaining tale of how it all came about was recounted many times. I was told by many of the guests that my practical joke had caused them to become more charitable to the poor veiled women standing by the gates. I felt pleased to have created generosity.

But since that innocent evening, I had become much more serious about the female lives being controlled by the Saudi culture, a male-controlled environment that gave little consideration to women's happiness.

The more injustice I saw, the more I felt an overwhelming compulsion to penetrate the awesome unknowns of the Saudi female life. What is it like to walk among fellow humans while nearly unrecognizable *as* a human being oneself? Does the veil neutralize *all* feelings of individuality? Does the veil dim *every* joy of life?

My intention is to spend the entire day and evening veiled. I will in the morning shop in the souk until *salat*, the mid-day prayer. After prayer, I will buy a few groceries in Spinney's supermarket, one of only two Western-style supermarkets in the city. After grocery shopping, and at the end of the lengthy sundown prayer, I plan to go veiled into my office.

A Lebanese guard I know at the hospital has agreed to meet me at the guard gate at a prearranged time so I can enter the grounds without undergoing the routine security check for all employees and visitors. I am in the swank hospital six days a week as a Western worker, but I want to view hospital activities through the eyes of a native veiled woman.

Since my planned activities are timed around the Islamic prayer schedules, I have already confirmed the prayer timetable in the English-language Arabic newspaper, *The Arab News*.

Soon after my arrival in the kingdom, I discover that the Islamic faith sets the agenda and tone of every aspect of public life, even for me, a Western Christian female visitor.

Most Westerners in Riyadh are uneasy because of the kingdom's strict adherence to religious law. However, the Saudis I personally know have never complained that their everyday lives are ruled by the tenets of the Islamic faith. Indeed, Saudis are rightfully proud that their ancestors were the first Muslims and that they are expected to fulfill important duties as the keepers and enforcers of the faith. Several Saudi friends routinely point out that it is "demanding" to be a good Muslim, while it is "easy" to be a practicing Christian.

Aware that the noontime call to prayer will signal the shopkeepers to shutter their storefronts, I discreetly push back the sleeve of the black cloak I am wearing, the *abaaya*, and glance at my watch. According to the prayer schedule, I have only two hours to browse the bazaar.

Covered from head to toe in my *abaaya*, along with the black veil and head scarf, not an inch of my white flesh is on view. Only the most pious Muslim women cover their hands and feet, but the skin of my hands and feet is so fair that to maintain the ruse, I have no choice but to wear black gloves and black stockings.

Certainly, the veil has one advantage. I can thoroughly inspect everyone around me without anyone seeing my impolite stares. I can even make naughty faces, if I am so inclined. Only in this regard, does the veil free the wearer.

The souk is packed with shoppers. Since Friday in Muslim countries is analogous to Sunday in the Christian world, Thursday in Riyadh is the same as Saturday in the West. The souk is filled with many veiled women enjoying a weekend shopping excursion.

Although lured inside by the wide variety of merchandise for sale, the black-veiled women encircling me are so slow in their movements that I fear they will cause a human pile-up. Occasionally a group of women pauses to lean against the shop counters or walls. I feel profound empathy for their desire to rest. Forced to fully cover in black in the desert heat of Riyadh, where temperatures climb above a hundred degrees Fahrenheit, who can blame them if they move as slowly as possible?

The heat of the closed souk is increasing. I unintentionally suck the gauzy fabric of the black veil into my mouth. The material wafts a pungent odor into my nostrils and leaves an unpleasant taste on my tongue.

With each tentative step, my legs grow twisted within the folds of the too-long black cloak. I've noticed that many Saudi women are tall and thin. The black cloaks are designed with their figures in mind. Unfortunately, I am a short woman, so all cloaks are too long. To keep from stumbling, I try to gather the fabric of my cloak and long dress in my right hand, to lift it above the dirt-worn pathway, but this awkward clutching only worsens the situation. When I stumble on a stone so jagged I feel its sharpness through my shoe leather, I have to bite my lip to keep from crying out.

I am having enormous difficulty seeing. I must peer through a black veil and every shopkeeper or item at which I gaze, and every face upon which I look appears dimmed in shadows. Distinguishing specific features is an ordeal.

Despite the difficulties, I linger to examine the glittering array of 18-and 21-karat-gold bracelets, chains and rings. While chains are hanging on the wall, bangles are perfectly lined up under glass cases. As is the case for most females in the kingdom, the stacks of golden jewelry never fail to tempt me.

I pause to examine some enticing wide bracelet bangles. From earlier experience, I know that each of the bangles bears individual patterns, but all details appear indistinct through the veil. I need to get closer. I bend over and lean near to the glass-topped counter.

No, being closer doesn't help. The Saudi shopkeeper quickly steps behind his counter to assist me. He speaks a few enthusiastic words in Arabic that I cannot understand, and in response, I make a sound without words.

I stand sideways and look down. No. Peering from either periphery is impossible. The veil is fastened to each side of my head while my head scarf loosely drapes over the veil.

"Hmmm..." I then shift my body from front to side several times to see if the view improves.

The shopkeeper is watchfully silent.

I try the front view once again. I bend forward. I am so close to the golden bangles that my nose touches the glass.

Intuitively, I feel the eyes of the shopkeeper studying me closely. Saudis are not naturally bold. He takes a step backward.

The only possibility for unrestricted sight is from the unfastened hem of the veil. Many times during the past months I observed Saudi women as they cautiously raised the bottom of their face veils to examine merchandise. I am not practiced in the fine art of subtle movement and fear that I might expose my face, which is bound to raise an alarm. A suspicious man might even summon the morals police.

But the bright gold bangles beckon.

The hem of my veil is tucked into my blouse, which is hidden beneath my cloak. I use my fingers to extricate the veil, but I pull too strongly and the hairpin that secures the right side of my veil falls to the ground.

Disaster! Without that pin my veil will swing loose from one side of my face, revealing my pale features. There is nothing to do but to find the hairpin.

As I stoop down, the shopkeeper peers over the top of the counter, and then, to my dismay, he gallantly comes around to assist me.

Holding the veil with my left hand, I pat the earthen floor with my right hand, frantically searching for that much-needed pin.

The shopkeeper's voice has a questioning tone as he squats beside me, once again speaking to me in Arabic.

Instinct tells me that he must be asking me what I have lost, so I grunt once again.

When the well-meaning man speaks the second time, I ever so slightly push my scarf back and point to the hairpin holding the secure side of my veil.

He understands my unspoken message and starts to rummage around with me.

Just when I am about to give up and consider my day's mission a failure, the shopkeeper begins to speak gleefully.

I squint as I peer through my veil.

The smiling shopkeeper holds the hairpin between his fingers and waves his hand triumphantly.

He talks happily as I secure my veil, but I do not speak. By now the poor man is likely convinced I am mute.

Feeling that he deserves a reward, I consider purchasing a gold bangle. Each bangle cost approximately 500 SR (US $150), depending on the bangle's weight and the customer's bargaining skill. I can't haggle if I can't speak, and I can only nod and gesture.

When I turn away with my new purchase, I slip and automatically say, "*Shukran*," the Arabic word for "thank you." With my southern American accented *shukran*, there is no mistaking that I am not a Saudi woman.

I turn and rush away as quickly as my confining garments allow.

"*Afwan!*" (Don't mention it!) he cries out in surprise.

I feel the man's questioning eyes upon me as I hurriedly create a distance between us.

When I round the corner I am panting. I stand quietly, waiting to see if I have been followed.

Within a few minutes I feel safe enough to readjust my cloak, veil, and head scarf.

As I stroll past the sandal makers, a Saudi woman accidentally tramples on the back hem of my cloak. No doubt she, like me, is having difficulty seeing. I hear the distinct sound of fabric rip and I am jerked to a full stop. I would topple backward, but the woman is tall and heavy-built and blocks my fall. I carefully gather the folds of my cloak and continue walking.

Truthfully, I am comically clumsy in the veil. How on earth can Saudi women endure wearing this cumbersome costume? And how can they do it with such elegant style?

I sigh but continue my stroll. I pause when I notice a squatting Bedouin woman selling loose nuts from a straw basket. The woman pauses to peer around the crowded souk. I guess correctly that she is about to lift her veil. I stand and watch as she deftly lifts the hem of her veil before taking a quick sip of canned orange soda. No bystander could possibly catch a glimpse of her forbidden face.

Even as I admire such a practiced movement, I cannot match it.

Suddenly I am overwhelmed by a rush of anger that any woman must wear a face veil. Truthfully, I am ready to fight *someone*. I look around angrily.

The Saudi men in the souk appear to be in good spirits, walking freely through the market while their subservient, veiled wives follow dutifully behind. They seem cool and comfortable in their loose white *thobes*, sandaled feet, and uncovered faces while their wives are wilting in their heavy black garments.

. Other Saudi men are standing or sitting in knotted groups, enthusiastically gossiping in the musical Arabic language while they watch the women in their circle. I know they are guarding their women like a shepherd guards his flock. The unseen danger they worry about is the possibility that a female in their family groups might commit some dishonorable act, such as having a conversation with a strange man, or lift their veils to display their faces.

Still other men sit idly on stools behind their golden wares, no doubt wishing that a wealthy Saudi woman will appear to buy a basket full of expensive trinkets.

Are these men truly contented with a life of guarding women to restrain them from innocent pastimes? Do they feel nothing for the plight of the black-veiled women in their midst? Even if their minds approve,

44

surely their hearts must feel shame at the unspeakable lives the women of their family are forced to live.

My emotions are spinning out of control. I begin to glare in all directions. Each time I catch a shadowy view of a Saudi male face through the black shroud that covers my face, I give the man an unseen fierce look.

The male shopkeepers continue to smile and point out their wares. Their efforts only spur my fury...until I realize dispiritedly that the men are wholly oblivious of my escalating anger.

When a young Saudi shopkeeper in one of the gold stalls speaks to me in Arabic and enthusiastically thrusts a heavily ornate 18-karat –gold breastplate toward my face, I grumble without words. I wave my black-gloved hands as though his golden products are beneath me.

Breathing heavily once again, I lean against the side of a wooden stall. The scent of the veil brushing against my nose and lips is so nauseating that the memory of the small shop where I purchased my veil and *abaaya* suddenly rushes back.

Bolts of cloth were piled high against the front windows. The only artificial light came from a single electric bulb swinging at the end of an unraveling cord. Even in the dismal light I could see grime on the counter surface and on the green and gray shaded linoleum floor.

The pleasant-faced Indian shopkeeper was polite, chirping a friendly greeting when I walked through the doorway.

He was cute as he laughingly slipped on an *abaaya* and face veil, teasingly pulling the veil on and off. I was startled to witness his ease at wearing female attire until I recalled that women are not allowed to try on clothes to determine a proper fit, when outside their homes. This male clerk has become accustomed to modeling female wares. He's quite the actor, prancing around the small shop. He forgets himself and begins to flirt, fluttering his eyes and speaking slowly, "The beauty of white faces should be seen, not covered."

I shrug at his nonsense before leaning forward to take the veil from his hands for a personal examination. I quickly purchased the items I needed and bolted from the shop. Remembering that I never bothered to wash any of my purchases, I recoil, dreading the diseases I might catch from the unwashed fabric. I quickly tighten my lips, breathing the stale air through my nose, cursing the face veil.

Chapter Seven
Souk Strolling

A man in a white *thobe* surprises me when he brushes my shoulder as he walks by. He stops, and then stands too close for conservative Riyadh.

I gasp, wondering how on earth I am going to discourage a flirty Saudi man when I can't even speak his language.

That's when I hear Peter Sasson merrily ask, his distinctive voice low, "Are you quite ready to leave now?"

I slowly exhale. The man in the *thobe* is my European boyfriend. In the months following our first date, Peter and I have become involved in an exclusive romantic relationship. Since that time, we have enjoyed a number of desert adventures.

My fears vanish. "No. I'm only resting for a minute." I pause. "It's so hot under this darn cloak I am about to burst into flames!"

Peter laughs.

He has obviously been watching very closely as he followed me throughout the souk.

We had agreed earlier that Peter would watch from a discreet distance and be ready to rescue me if I required his assistance. The day's adventure has been so overpowering that I have forgotten him.

Peter is the perfect "undercover agent" for this outing. With his smooth olive skin, dark brown hair and ability to speak Arabic, he can pass for a handsome light-skinned Arab with a European education. When wearing the Saudi *thobe* and *shamagh* he looks rather dashing.

47

An international man, Peter was an only child to his parents and was raised in Alexandria, Egypt, where the Sasson family had settled to become wealthy cotton plantation owners. Peter was then educated in an exclusive school in England, and lived in France and Italy before traveling to Saudi Arabia. He arrived in the kingdom the year before I accepted a position at the hospital. Self-assured and resourceful, he is willing to take on any exciting exploit.

"Take care, then," Peter said before warning me, "I saw a *mutawah* walking in a side alley."

A *mutawah*! I look left and right.

Even in 1979, when the kingdom is filled with Western working expatriates, the *Mutawain* remain uncompromising clergymen who cling to their role of policing public morals throughout Arabia. I had made the discovery early on that even the ruling royal family can do little to curb the barbaric behavior of the *Mutawain*. This inability to act is partially fueled out of fear that the powerful clerics will call for the royals downfall from the loudspeakers mounted on the towers of the kingdom's neighborhood mosques. In order to keep the al-Saud family secure on their throne, Saudis and foreigners alike must endure relentless scrutiny from these inflexible men.

The *Mutawain* are fearsome opponents. Since arriving in the kingdom, Peter and I have both suffered unpleasant experiences at the hand of these angry men of religion.

I pat at my veil and scarf to make certain that none of my hair has escaped my black coverings. The *Mutawain* will not wink at my deception.

When I hear the conspicuous shouts of a *mutawah* mingled with the cries of women from a nearby street, I decide to leave the area.

I study the figures in *thobes* around me, searching for Peter. Then I recognize him conspicuously staring at my feet. He is checking my identity by inspecting my

48

shoes. This morning he had tied a small colored ribbon onto the black strap of my shoe, a trick we had heard was routine in Saudi life.

"I don't want to lose track of you and grab the wrong woman," he said, and had laughed. "It would be off with my head!"

As I stroll in front of him, I nod my head and whisper, "Let's leave this place."

Peter speaks without looking at me. "Where now?"

"The Bedouin souk."

This Bedouin souk, or antiques market, is a favorite with many expatriates. No souk is more evocative of Saudi Arabia's past. And for some unheard of reason, the *Mutawain* seldom harass women in this area.

The Bedouin souk is a maze of alleys off Uthman ibn Affan Street. Many times during the past year, Peter and I have spent enjoyable hours browsing through the open stalls where daggers, coffee pots, incense-burners, camel bags, and antique weapons are on jumbled display.

The likelihood that my hands were stroking old muskets used in the days of Bedouin tribal raiding parties never failed to create electrifying images in my mind.

Prior to my arrival in Saudi Arabia, I had mistakenly believed that all Saudis were Bedouin. I quickly discovered that there is a marked difference between settled city Arabs and nomadic Bedouin Arabs. These two groups have long distrusted and disliked each other.

The educated Saudis I know at the royal hospital routinely scorn and ridicule the Bedouin and act embarrassed to be connected to this mainly uneducated facet of their society.

The Bedouin way of life has changed little since the time of Prophet Muhammad, (Peace be upon him) the founder of the Islamic faith. These proud people feel that their own lifestyle is superior to that of the urban dwellers, or "Godless sinners," as the Bedouin call them.

There were times that the Bedouin refused to enter the settled interior communities of Arabia without first stuffing cotton or cloth into their nostrils, asserting that their city brethren had an obnoxious odor.

Although Bedouins can be found throughout the kingdom, there are only three places where they are likely to feel comfortable enough to mingle with foreign visitors. Restraints are loosened in the Bedouin's own desert encampments, which can be found in various desert areas throughout the kingdom, at the camel souk, located on the outskirts of Saudi cities, and at the Bedouin souk, where Peter and I are now entering.

Chapter Eight
Bedouin Chick Malaak

Just as Peter and I enter the souk, an old Bedouin woman beckons to me. Like the other women, she is selling homemade wares, but she seems to be quite the businesswoman and is sitting slightly apart from the others. In front of her is a display of handmade silver jewelry and cans of orange soda, which is the favored beverage of the Bedouin.

Thirsty, I stop and dig through my small handbag for two riyals, which I offer to her.

When she hands me the soda, I notice that her fingers are worn and that her thumbs are huge and out of shape.

I've been told that the Bedouin women are responsible for much of the routine work of Bedouin life, including caring for and setting up the goat-hair tents. Such difficult work would certainly disfigure fingers and thumbs.

I accept the soda and lift the hem of my veil slightly to sip the warm liquid.

Her Bedouin veil style is unlike my own. While my entire face, including my eyes, is covered by black cloth, her eyes are revealed. Her black eyes flash character.

Her cloak is old and frayed along the edges. She is a true Bedouin woman, with hennaed hands and calloused feet that show from below her floor-length *abaaya*. The country's oil wealth has not trickled down to her.

I am eager to ask this woman many questions. Once again I silently berate myself for not speaking Arabic.

She and I exchange long stares of curiosity. I know with an unexplained certainty that she senses I am not who I pretend to be. She knows that I am an impostor. Is it the manner in which I drape my scarf or veil? Is it the way I hold my cloak?

Accustomed from puberty to the complete veil, Saudi women exhibit a distinct grace, holding their cloaks firmly in place with poise and style.

I feel a surge of joy as I see the wrinkles tighten around her eyes, the only part of her face I can see.

She is smiling.

With her encouraging smile, I am moved to recklessness. I *must* talk to this woman! I motion for Peter to come forward. He will translate.

Peter Sasson is a rare man who has mastered his emotions, taking every man and woman as he finds them, without attaching his expectations to their beliefs and behavior. While he often claims I am more emotional and melodramatic than even the dramatic Italians he knows, he appears to enjoy our dissimilarities.

He watches my swathed face as if he can see it.

I catch a small flicker of amusement as I explain. "Peter, I've *got* to talk to this woman. Tell her who I am, and..." I pause. I must think of a credible reason for veiling. The truth might offend her. My words come in a rush. "Tell her that I veiled out of respect. Tell her that I wish to speak with her."

I can see Peter's big grin. He dips his head in agreement. "All right, then."

Peter squats to the ground. He bunches his *thobe* under his legs and stares at the woman for brief moment. He then speaks slowly in Arabic.

I'm happy to see that he carries his Saudi prayer beads in his right hand.

Peter explains the situation to the woman, asking if she will talk with me.

The Bedouin woman looks from Peter to me. I am a veiled woman in a souk in Saudi Arabia. She is most likely questioning why I need a translator.

The lines around her eyes loosen and I know she is no longer smiling.

The barriers of custom and religion threaten the encounter before it begins.

"Is she a Muslim?" she asks in a demanding tone.

"*La. La.*" (No. No.) He then puts forth the argument all good Muslims understand. "She believes in the same God, and your God is one God for the Muslims and the Christians."

She gives a slight nod at Peter's words. She continues to stare.

On impulse I lift the front of my veil and show her my American face.

The lines around her eyes tighten once more. She is smiling again.

I understand this Bedouin woman is unique when she pats the ground with her hand. She is inviting a stranger to share her mat.

I throw my veil over my head and sit. Several Saudi men stare at my unveiled face, but they do not move in our direction. None of the men are *Mutawain*, so I am safe. Should a religious man witness a veiled woman tossing aside her veil, she would be singled out for attack. These men probably assume that I am the foreign wife of a non-Saudi Muslim.

Peter continues to squat, prepared to translate.

I learn that her name is Malaak, which she proudly proclaims, means "Angel."

First I must answer Malaak's questions.

Leaning toward Peter while keeping her eyes on my face, she wants to know where I come from, what am I doing in her country, and what is the *true* reason I am veiling.

53

Malaak startles me when she reaches out and squeezes my arm with her hand.

"Too skinny," she declares.

Peter laughs, telling me her words.

She lightly brushes my face with her hennaed hand.

"Too white," she exclaims, then asks Peter. "Why did you wed a female too small to give you healthy sons? There are many strong Bedouin who can fill your home with children."

Peter laughs a second time.

I don't take offense, as this is a polite controversy. Within a short while of arriving in the kingdom, I listened courteously as Saudis politely informed me that large, robust women give birth to tall, healthy sons. At five foot and two inches tall and weighing one hundred and ten pounds, I am not up to their physical standards for top quality human reproduction.

With a twinkle in her eyes, she directs her next question to me and waits patiently while Peter translates.

"Tell me. Why do you veil?"

This wise Bedouin woman has quickly seen through me. I decide to tell her the truth.

My words come from Peter's mouth.

"I am from a country where women do not veil," I confess. "I felt drawn to live your life. To know how it feels to live under the veil."

She nods with a new force, believing I am envious. "The Bedouin life is best."

"I wish to know your Bedouin life."

"What is it you do not know?" Her voice carries a shade of surprise, as though she believes the Bedouin life is well-known throughout the world.

"Everything." I pause. "Your childhood." Yes, I would start at the beginning. "What do you remember of your childhood?"

She sits silently for a brief time.

54

How I long to see her full face, to sit freely as companions, discovering all there is to know about the other. Given the opportunity, I know in my heart that we could become devoted friends.

She begins to speak slowly. "I was the oldest of many children. I remember small things of the early life. There is a picture of my father's tent in my mind. It was made of black goat hair. Six poles kept it upright. I liked to swing around those poles. My mother was always cooking. I remember a sweet taste of goat meat and rice. I remember the goats and the camels." Malaak is smiling once again, pleased to entertain me. "That's what I remember."

"You say the Bedouin life is the best life. What was the best for you?"

She does not hesitate. "The family. The family was the best. The desert brings a family close. There are goats to be tended, meals to be cooked, tents to be mended, and water to be found. My father watched the sky for clouds. When rain clouds appeared, we took down our tent and gathered our livestock and followed the clouds across the desert."

I know that the term Bedouin means "people of the desert." The harsh conditions of desert nomadic life produced a unique people who had a fierce love for the desert, despite its brutalities. This Bedouin woman displays every unique aspect of the prideful Bedouin character that I had previously imagined.

I now come to the sensitive questions. I edge closer to Malaak.

"When did you have to start veiling?"

Her black eyes narrow under her veil. "My mother veiled. All the women veiled." She shrugged. "I wanted to veil. So I took the veil early, when I around eight years old."

"Eight? You *wanted* to veil at age eight? You were just a child."

Her eyes flash with pride. "Veiling is an honorable custom."

This is not what I expected her to say. I want to hear that she detests the veil.

Her next revelation startles me more. "I was the favorite child of my father."

"More than his sons?"

"I was my father's pet."

Disbelief sweeps over me. Surely this Bedouin woman has lived a life of deceptive euphoria, believing that she was the preference of her father, even over coveted sons.

"And marriage? Were you forced to wed?"

She laughs aloud. "The day of my wedding was a burst of glory. My father killed two young camels and six fat sheep. All the women in my tribe gathered in my father's tent to make me even more beautiful than I was."

She pauses, remembering. "My husband said that I was a gift from God. When he first saw my face his tongue could not move. He claimed that my beauty almost stopped his heart and put him under the sands, into an early grave."

Desperate to expose the hypocrisies and humiliations of Saudi female life, I hopefully ask, "Then, after you were married, did he beat you?"

She laughs once more. "Beat me? Never! He was a poet!"

Poetry enjoys such popularity among Arabs that poets in Saudi society acquire great influence. Practically every Saudi man I know is an aspiring poet.

"He was a poet." I repeat numbly.

Her voice rises slightly. "Yes, a poet." She pokes my arm with her finger. "My husband did not beat the females in his tent." She chuckled, "He wrote them poems."

I fret under her knowing stare, speaking lowly. "Poems. He wrote poems."

At my look of disappointment, her eyes mirror amusement. She volunteers. "Here is my favorite."

Peter falters as he translates. Although he grew up in Egypt and spoke good Arabic as a child, the years of living in Europe without Arabic friends, have taken a toll on his Arabic language skills. Additionally, there are notable differences between Egyptian Arabic and Saudi Arabic. I can see that Peter is struggling.

Malaak repeats the poem several times to make certain her words are understood.

"The black veils of Arabia hide her from all eyes.
She is my secret, revealed only to me.
She is my rain cloud.
By God! I dream of her eyes, locked on my face!
There was no thought before her.
There will be emptiness without her.
My black-veiled woman!"

The blend of Malaak's musical voice combined with the swaying of her covered head is almost hypnotizing.

After Peter roughly translated, she looks at me expectantly.

I compliment her husband's talents. "That was lovely."

She grunts with satisfaction.

I look around the souk. "Where is this poet?

"Dead. For many years."

"Oh. I am sorry."

"No. I am an old woman, soon forty-three years on this earth. Besides, who am I to question God?"

I try to hide my surprise. From what I could see of the flesh around her eyes, I had judged her age to be no less than sixty-five years old.

I want her to lift her veil so that I can see her entire face but I don't dare make such a request. This Bedouin woman would be deeply offended at the idea.

"What happened to your husband, the poet?"

"An accident."

"Accident?"

She quickly explains. "One day my husband traveled with three other men to a small village to trade goatskins and camel bags for sweet water and food in a can. They visited a family in that village. This family had a musket gun left behind by the Turks from the time of war and the small round pellets to put inside the gun. Some men were sitting by the coffee fire admiring the musket when a young boy picked up the long thread that holds the pellets, and for some reason only known to God, tossed the pellets into the fire! One man was killed. That man was my husband."

"Oh my. How dreadful! I am sorry."

She is touched by my sympathy. She pats my gloved hand. "I have had my happiness. I am content." She stares straight into my eyes and whispers, "My husband seems dead to everyone else, but he is not dead to me."

At that juncture, I instinctively remove my black gloves and stroke her hennaed hands. This Bedouin woman is only eleven years older than me, but her hands tell a tale of hardship and premature aging.

I take a deep breath.

"Peter. Thank her for telling me about her life. Tell her that my knowledge has grown because of her."

She nods her head several times.

She then turns to Peter and dispenses sound advice. "It is all right to keep this wife for her sweet beauty. But take a second wife for size and strength—a strong woman who can give you many strong sons."

I'm smiling when I stand. Pulling the veil back over my face, I say my goodbyes once again. Malaak and I part and then Peter and I begin walking through the souk to Peter's parked automobile.

I try to unravel my confusion. With my own eyes, I have seen and I know the blatant discriminations against women in Saudi Arabia. By my Western standards, every female heart in Saudi Arabia should be spilling over with misery. Yet I have just met a woman who has lived her entire life behind the veil, and she feels she has lived a better life than my own. Of course, she has no knowledge of the female freedoms so cherished in my Western world.

After moments of consideration, I feel a surprising spark of gladness. I'm relieved that Malaak has lived a good life, a happy life.

Peter is walking ahead of me, and forgetting my need for secrecy, I speak loudly. "It is good that Malaak does not know about women's freedoms."

Peter grunts and gives an indifferent shrug.

"She simply cannot imagine a life different from the one she has lived. If she could, she would rebel," I say with assurance.

"Right," Peter responds.

Yes, I am truly glad that Malaak is a satisfied woman and is happy living under the black veil of Arabia. Since change will not come to her life, I am thankful she is unaware of anything more.

As Peter and I walk along the main street to our parked automobile, I hear an alarming confrontation between a *mutawah* and two Filipina women. With a raised stick poised menacingly, the man is angrily shouting.

I study the women's attire. They are both dressed modestly. The only issue that might raise his stick is their uncovered hair. But I know that foreign women working in Saudi Arabia are told by their employers that there is no requirement for them to wear a head scarf and *abaaya*. But the religious clerics have their own ideas on the subject, and opinions vary from one cleric to another.

Foreign women really do not know what to do to discourage *Mutawain* attacks.

The two women are weeping and alternatively crying out.

"We are not Muslim, sir!" "We are not Muslim!"

I am grateful to see that the *mutawah* is accompanied by a city police office. In an effort to control the violent reactions of the religious zealots, the royals have had the wisdom to attach one regular police officer to each *mutawah*. The police officer will save these young women from a public thrashing, although there will be consequences if the religious clerics press the issue. Both will probably lose their jobs and be deported back to their country.

When he leads the two women to his squad car I overhear the policeman tell them in English that he is arresting them for indecent exposure.

Meanwhile the women around me—the veiled Saudis as well as foreign women—are moving away from the silent, still *mutawah*. When the policeman drives away, the *mutawah* will be free to terrorize any woman he chooses.

Peter and I stand and watch, speculating what poor female will next incur his wrath. Dressed as the most pious Saudi woman, with black gloves and stockings covering all my flesh, I do not feel in danger of his attention.

As Peter and I go on our way, my mind is full of activity as I question whether I will ever fully understand the impenetrable mysteries of life for women living in the Kingdom of Saudi Arabia.

Chapter Nine
The Wild *Mutawah*

When I arrived in the kingdom, I was told that as a non-Muslim woman I was not required to veil or even cover my hair. Of course, I was cautioned to be modest in dress. Despite the heat of Riyadh, there would be no sleeveless dresses or summer shorts.

I quickly discovered that the official government policy was poles apart from reality. The sight of an unveiled female face and blonde hair was a potential riot-causing event in the crowded streets of Riyadh. In fact, my uncovered blonde hair had caused a disturbance in the jewelry souk shortly after arriving in the kingdom. Since that dangerous moment, I had been careful to braid my long hair and to cover it with a black scarf.

Foreign women also inflamed the zealots in charge of public morals. To the despair of every woman living in the kingdom, these angry men had recently discovered the joys of spray paint. With flaming red beards and eyes glaring with hatred, *Mutawain* men traumatized shoppers by spraying red paint on female offenders of the faith.

I will never forget the day that I witnessed such an attack.

Only in the kingdom for a few months, I did not feel comfortable shopping alone. Peter instructed his Filipino office driver, Joe, to remain with me while his part-time Pakistani maid, Majida, and I shopped. I was in the market for a camera so we would go to the Batha souk, on the corner of al Batha and al Khazzam Street. The last thing on my mind was the danger of a roving *mutawah* for I was dressed modestly in an ankle-length dress with my long hair braided and hidden under my scarf and cloak. My face was on view for passing shoppers to see, but no Western women were expected to wear the face veil, so I felt safe.

Since Majida is Muslim, she was discreetly attired in a skirt that hung four or five inches above her ankles. Her arms were exposed from the elbows down, but I thought nothing of it since Majida is so petite that she looks like a teenager. The fabric on her head scarf was rather sheer, but the scarf was black and her hair was black, so with black layered on black, there was nothing for anyone to see. Majida's face was uncovered, but many Muslim women from neighboring countries do not always cover their faces, as the Saudi women do.

I felt that we were both well within the strict dress code required for females by Saudi society.

Joe strolled a few feet behind us while Majida and I window shopped. We were walking calmly past a dim alley when a human figure sprang up then swooshed down in front of us.

It was a *mutawah*. As a result of the unexpected shock, we both screamed. With a loud, angry cry, the man covered Majida's arms with red spray paint.

The man's face was deeply lined and his beard was henna-dyed. I was amazed that although noticeably old in years, he was young in body and spirit. It was as though the *mutawah* was attached to a powerful spring! I had never seen anyone but a professional athlete who had the ability to bound to such heights. His leaps were so forceful that his checkered headdress actually flapped in the air, reminding me of giant rabbit ears. Had we not been the focus of his demented attention, the incident would have been comical.

Still springing up and down, he began circling us, spraying Majida with red paint. Once or twice he dipped low enough to spray her legs before bounding into the air once again.

"*Help!*" I shouted. Eager for male assistance, I glanced behind me, searching for Joe. To my dismay, I saw Joe rapidly running away.

Only moments before, the busy street had hummed with shoppers, but the street had now emptied.

On his final leap, the crazed man reached out and pinched Majida's arm hard enough to bruise the flesh to bone.

Majida screeched in pain.

Standing motionless for the first time, the *mutawah* began to shout angrily.

I stood in amazement.

The *mutawah* was so enraged that the wrinkles on his face began to rise and fall with his words.

Too late, I was able to find my voice. I shouted in English, "*Stop it!* What is your problem? We are properly dressed!"

The *mutawah* looked at me for the first time.

My tone of voice, combined with a white face appeared to astonish him.

My heart was pounding but I tried to look forceful.

The man's piercing eyes were suddenly filled with intense hatred. It was my first occasion to look into the eyes of someone who plainly wanted to physically harm me.

I braced myself for the spray of paint that was sure to come.

Much to my surprise and relief, the *mutawah* turned his back and walked away as calmly as if the incident had never happened.

"My God!" My entire body was tingling from the shock of the attack. "Majida! Are you all right?"

Poor Majida was making low, whimpering noises. She was rubbing her red-coated arms and hands. During the frenzied attack her face had been sprayed as well.

"Madam Jean, Madam Jean..." Majida burst into heaving sobs.

I grabbed her tiny hand and we began to stumble toward our parked car.

Heads appeared as shoppers peeked from the shop fronts. No one offered a gesture of sympathy.

I saw Joe lurking behind our automobile, so frightened that his face was pale and his eyes stretched open wide.

I bit my tongue, deciding not to rebuke him. Filipinos are routinely treated as one of the weak groups in the Saudi society, rarely enjoying mentors to protect them. Had Joe openly confronted the *mutawah*, he would probably have been flogged and then deported.

I suddenly felt a rush of shame. I should have reacted sooner. My lame excuse was that the attack had been so sudden that I was too stunned to counter the assault.

❧

I shiver, forcing my thoughts to the present moment. I glance at Peter who is now calmly smoking a cigarette while studying camera equipment displayed in a glass case.

When the police car passes by, I look inside to see the two Filipino women. With heads in their hands, both are weeping, humiliated at being attacked and arrested.

Poor, poor women! They are as traumatized as the unfortunate Majida had been. Majida left the kingdom within days of the assault. When I pleaded with her to stay, knowing that she was returning to a life of certain poverty, she swore that, "I would rather starve in my poor village than live the life of a woman in Saudi Arabia."

Remembering the day she left, I am brushed by a great sorrow.

"Let's get out of here," I tell Peter.

My brief experience wearing the veil has been searing. I do not have to witness yet another injustice to grasp that female life under the black veils of Riyadh can be terrifying.

Despite Malaak's positive view of the veil, I *know* that most non-Bedouin women in Saudi Arabia do not share her views. And I know that as long as a single woman on earth is veiled against her will, I will always carry the weight of an invisible veil on my own shoulders.

Chapter Ten
Riyadh Chick Nayam

With my roommates away for the evening, I wander aimlessly through our small apartment. Disheartened after my experiences beneath the veil today, I have fallen into a rare depression. I am more aware than ever of the dark reality that much of the world can be a dangerous place for the female sex.

I pace, silently questioning: Is there anything I can do to change the destiny of veiled women? Truthfully, it feels presumptuous to even think this way. The situation is too complex and traditions are too deeply rooted for any one person, and particularly a foreigner, to make a difference.

I am suddenly struck by the only possible solution. Saudi women are the answer to their own problems! Saudi women must lead the charge. There are many wealthy, educated and intelligent women in the country, but all are hiding behind the black veils. Native women must transform and overturn the regulations and rules that have nothing to do with Islam yet are sanctioned by this male-intoxicated country.

Change must make its way through the cities and into the desert by the efforts of Saudi women. While I cannot lead this effort, I can encourage Saudi women I meet to embrace the boldness necessary to bring action. Perhaps I can be the hand swinging the sword of change.

My new ideas lighten my mood.

The following weekend while visiting Peter, I confide my new idea. "Peter, from this day forward, I'll make a special effort to befriend Saudi woman. I'll persuade Saudi women to push for change." I smile and nod my head, tapping my foot on the floor in cadence with my words. "Never again will I refuse an invitation to a Saudi home or to a woman's party."

Westerners are new to the kingdom and helping to modernize Saudi Arabia. Native Saudis have not yet wearied of our presence. Hospitality is a trait deeply ingrained in the Saudi tradition, and many in the educated Saudi population welcome both Americans and Europeans into their country and into their homes. And, thanks to Dr. Feteih[6] and Peter, I have more opportunities to socialize with Saudis than do most Westerners.

Despite a persistent veil of intolerance directed against women, that is adversely coloring my personal experience in this desert kingdom, there is no denying that many Saudis are bright, lovely people whom I believe are secretly open to the idea of cultural and political change. From my personal observations, I have seen that most Saudis work around the issues that life has dealt them, while waiting for true change to begin at the top and work its way down to the masses.

I fear that they are waiting in vain.

"Yes. I'll seek out these women, Peter. If all the women of Saudi Arabia band together, they can be an explosive force."

"Forget it, darling. So long as the middle class makes buckets of money and the *Mutawain* are given free rein to attack women, men will not allow their women to revolt."

"I don't know."

I continue my talk with Peter, trying to persuade him that he might become involved, that he should convince his Saudi business friends to rise up in anger on behalf of their women. He needs to speak out, to tell them

---

[6] For a photo of Dr. Feteih, please visit
http://jeansasson.com/books/american-chick-gallery.html

that it is better for the country, and better for business to treat women as equal partners. By not allowing Saudi women's participation in public and business life, the Saudis are squandering half of their national human resources.

Peter laughs gently at my naïveté, and says as he walks away. "Leave me out of your schemes to change the world. Live and let live, I say."

Peter's attitude disappoints me. But I am not willing to give up. Change, I realize, is going to happen only if Saudi women insist upon it. And I am perfectly positioned to encourage their subversive inclinations. From now on, I decide, I will accept every invitation to female social functions, and I will take advantage of every opportunity.

❧

Several weeks later, I am alone in my office in the Medical Affairs Department sorting papers when I hear a thump outside my office door. Moments later, whimpering noises bring me to my feet.

Nearly every Saudi male entering the hospital as a patient, or as the relative of a patient, requests to meet with Dr. Nizar Feteih, a well known Saudi who is the head of the hospital. Saudis who know him, or who have heard of his accomplishments, are understandably proud of the Saudi doctor. To protect Dr. Feteih's privacy, Medical Affairs offices are tucked away on the hospital's second floor.

I walk into the hallway and see nothing of interest. I peer to the right down the corridor leading to the hospital administrative offices. Everyone seems to be going about their usual routines.

I turn to my left to the hallway leading to the Medical Records department. A large bundle near the women's restroom catches my eye. "Now what is this?" I

68

mutter. It is July and so hot that many of the hospital employees schedule vacations during this time. Even Dr. Feteih is away, visiting King Khalid at his summer palace in Taif. At this same time, the deputy medical director is on a short leave.

This is something I'll have to deal with alone. First I try to open the restroom door, but it is locked.

I lean forward to inspect the bundle on the floor. I step back when the blanket stirs and a whimpering noise escapes. I lean forward once again and hesitantly push the blanket aside.

I gasp as I step back. There is a baby in the blanket. I take a deep breath and step forward. The baby's head is oversized and misshapen, with its little features pitifully scrunched in the center of its face.

I fall back against the wall, my heart pounding. Even though I've lived in the kingdom for only a short while, I've learned that Saudis born handicapped have an extraordinarily difficult life.

The customs of the Bedouin still influence modern Saudi life. Meager resources cannot be wasted on those without the ability to contribute favorably to the tribe. Such babies are often neglected in the hope they will quickly succumb to illness and die.

Has this sick baby been abandoned by its parents?

I must do something, so I lift the little one from the floor and into my arms. I try to cuddle the over-sized bundle against my chest while making soothing noises. The infant begins to make heaving sobs. I decide to take the baby to one of our pediatrics outpatient clinics. Handicapped by a big head, I assume that the baby was brought in for treatment. Surely someone in the clinic will have information on this child.

Just as I am rounding the corner to leave the area, I hear a yelp of distress. I turn back to see a veiled woman with upraised arms rushing at me. *"Ahlan!"* (Hello!) I shout a greeting in my elementary Arabic.

69

The woman is moving so fast that her veil and *abaaya* both flutter. It is clear that this woman is the mother of the baby.

She comes to a sudden stop, startling me when she shouts in accented but perfect English, "You have my baby!"

Relieved, I smile and place the baby in her outstretched arms, explaining, "I was afraid this baby had been abandoned. I was taking it to the nurse's station in pediatrics."

I know she is staring at me from under that black veil which totally covers her face. I strain to speak normally, although I'm speaking to the equivalent of a blank wall.

"You left your baby on the floor?" I prompt.

She defends herself in perfect English. "Never would I leave my baby! After seeing the doctor and hearing his sad news, I became dizzy with grief. I went to the toilet. I left my baby only a short distance from the door."

She is beginning to sob as she asks, "Do you have a place I can sit? For only a moment?"

It is extremely rare for any Saudi to seek comfort from a Westerner. In the age-old tradition of Bedouin hospitality and generosity, the Saudis I know are warm and friendly, yet much time and many efforts are required before actual confidences are shared.

I feel true sympathy for her situation, the mother of a special needs baby. I guide her from the hall to a chair by my desk and pour her a glass of water.

With her sobbing baby clutched to her chest, she begins to weep in earnest, and I quickly close and lock the door.

To my surprise she lifts her veil and pats it securely over her head.

I stare openly. I have never once looked at a veiled woman when I did not long to see her face, hear her voice, and know her personal story. Many times I have thrust one hand into the other to keep from reaching out and pulling the veil up and away.

Her face carries a clue to her character. The softness of her eyes conveys a distinctive sweetness. She cannot be called beautiful, but she is very pretty, with fair skin and delicate features. Her hair and eyes are brilliantly dark. Her hair falls in ringlets upon her shoulders. She is still cloaked, so I can only imagine her physique, but she appears slight. She is wearing a thin gold chain around her small neck.

Her searching eyes look at me.

I smile with encouragement and find the nerve to place my hand lightly on her shoulder.

My compassionate gesture causes her to burst anew into tears. While sobbing, she stretches her arms out so that I can look at her baby's face. "This is my fourth child! Three are already in the grave. Poor Shaker has lived three miserable months!" She shakes her head vigorously. "He will die soon, just like the others."

Over the next hour, I learn her tragic story.

Nayam is an educated woman. In 1975 she earned her degree at a well-known university in Beirut, Lebanon.

Before 1977, Saudi women were permitted the freedom to travel abroad for their advanced education. But in 1977, an al-Saud family crisis, brought about by royal adultery, led to the public execution of Princess Misha'il, granddaughter of Prince Mohammed, the eldest living son in the al-Saud family. Her lover, Khalid Muhalhal, the nephew of the special Saudi envoy to Lebanon, was beheaded.

In reaction to the humiliation of al-Saud adultery, and the international scandal revolving around public executions for the crime of unsanctioned sex, King Khalid decreed that all Saudi women were banned from traveling abroad without a "*Mahram*"-a close male relative, such as a father or brother, to whom the female is forbidden to marry-as an escort.

Since few fathers or brothers are willing or able to take years out of their lives to accompany a daughter or sister abroad, virtually all Saudi women have stopped being educated abroad.

Nayam is one of the lucky few who left prior to the confining royal decree.

She tells me, "My parents are highly educated. Both of them. They are free-thinkers. My father was educated in Lebanon. He met my mother there. She has Syrian roots. They fell in love in a normal way. Their mistake was to come back to my father's country. I am one of six children. I grew up in Jeddah, thanks be to God. I did not even cover my face, unless the men of religion were on a mission."

A tight smile pauses briefly on her lips.

I nod. It is well known that women are not as restricted in Jeddah as they are in rigid Riyadh. Such a thing would never happen in Riyadh, the most conservative of all Saudi cities where all Saudi women veil. No wonder Nayam is quick to toss the veil over her head.

"My parents encouraged all their children to get a degree, even their three daughters." She smiles proudly. "I earned my dentistry degree easily." She sighs, "I planned to work as a pediatric dentist. All my patients would be children, so there would be no cause for complaint from my husband."

At the thought of her husband, Nayam weeps quietly. "I did not complain when my parents arranged for me to meet a cousin, a cousin they wanted me to marry. This is our way." She sighs again. "My fiancée's name was Obeid."

I pull up a chair and sit near her.

"I even met him before we married."

She looks into the distance, a frown on her face. "Obeid is not handsome, but I found him to be intelligent and interesting. He owns several contracting firms, and when we met he had been awarded a government contract to build a high school in the kingdom. In the beginning, Obeid seemed pleased and proud that his educated wife wanted to have a career. He even sketched a building design for my new office."

She pauses to take a sip of water and to kiss her baby's little lips. "I ignored an early troubling indicator of things to come. Obeid's draft drawing of the dental clinic had separate rooms for male and female children."

In Saudi Arabia, male and female children are sometimes allowed to freely mingle socially until puberty. Although adult Saudis are sex-segregated in almost every setting, they seldom insist on the separation of young children by sex, unless they are of the most conservative tribes.

"He was so nice...at first. When I told him that I did not want to wear the veil, he stared at me. When I asked him if he could find anything in his Muslim faith that required women to cover their faces, he smiled without commenting. When I told him that I wanted to wait a few years to have children, he smiled without speaking.

"The day after our wedding, Obeid sat me down, talking in his soft voice, telling me that he wanted a wife who stayed at home, a wife who would give him children, a wife who wanted a husband to be a real man and take care of his family. I protested that I wanted to pursue the career I had trained for, and that my work as a dentist would be ideal for a wife and mother. I could make my own hours, I told him.

"But Obeid reminded me that he was the husband, the head of our family, and that I was never to question his decisions. I was to put the thought of a career out of my mind.

"When Obeid learned that I did not own a veil to cover my face and eyes, he called his mother and asked her to meet us at the Riyadh airport with veil in hand. When I protested, he softly told me that my exposed face would cause a scandal. "You must cover your face when you leave our home," he ordered in a gentle voice.

"When I wept in our bed, Obeid demanded his marital rights again and again, asking me, what woman could want more than what I am offering? Everyone was happy, but me, when I became pregnant on our honeymoon."

Nayam haltingly reveals that her first child, a son, died before his first birthday. His kidneys did not function properly. With such a small amount of urine output, his entire body was slowly poisoned. The infant had suffered terribly with gruesome raw red rashes that coated his body. The rashes developed into open sores that sometimes oozed pus and blood. Even Nayam, his loving mother, admitted that she believed his death merciful.

Her second child, a daughter, died within six months with the exact medical problems her brother suffered. The poor darling had left her earthly life whimpering with pain.

After the death of their second child, Nayam's physician recommended genetic screening and counseling. Once the results were studied, Obeid and Nayam were cautioned by Western physicians not to have more children. They were told that both carried a gene that, when combined, was likely to cause terminal abnormalities in their offspring.

Many tribes in Saudi Arabia routinely marry within the tribe, with cousins marrying cousins on a regular basis. There is a belief that such customs strengthen families. Weakness comes from outside the family unit. The idea that medical dangers may lurk in intermarriage is an outlandish concept to most Saudis.

Obeid had scornfully rejected the warnings, insisting they try yet again. "Only God can decide this issue," Obeid declared.

Nayam's third child, a son, died within nine months of the same medical disorder.

Obeid insisted on yet more children. The grieving Nayam was pregnant within a week of burying her third child.

An exhausted Nayam pleaded with Obeid to take a second wife. Let another woman give him children, she implored. If he did not want two wives at the same time, she would not protest a divorce.

My jaw drops in surprise. The biggest fear of every Saudi woman I've met is that their spouse will bring a second wife into their lives. None that I ever heard of encouraged her husband to take a second wife.

"Obeid had no interest in another woman. Instead, he was angered by my suggestion. My husband became obsessed, telling me with that quiet voice that he could and would father a healthy child with me."

She lifts her chin, staring at the bundle in her arms. "Then my little Shaker was born with a head too large for his body. The doctors are doing what they can, but Shaker's head keeps growing. Even the head drain did little to stop it.

"Just today, the physician told Obeid we should not have any more babies. The doctor said in his medical opinion that all our babies will die prematurely."

She tells me that Obeid had spoken softly in that deadly voice of his, "Allah will decide."

"When I heard my husband's words, I knew that I would start screaming and never stop. I scooped up my child and ran away. I ran in the first elevator that opened and stepped out where it stopped. That is how I came to be here," she says, gesturing at the door and hallway.

Nayam's unmasked face glistens with fear. "I cannot change my husband's mind. About anything. Obeid is like a mountain between me and happiness."

"What about your parents? Can they help you?"

"Nothing." She looked into her baby's face and gave him a brief, faint smile. "They can do nothing. Both of my parents tried to speak with Obeid, but he froze them with his words." She hums the words, "Pleasing words filled with poison."

My thoughts are racing. I know that I would divorce this Obeid, but things are not so simple in Saudi Arabia. While divorce is an uncomplicated matter for Saudi men, it quickly becomes tangled with intricate complexities when it is the woman who wants a divorce.

Saudi men can divorce their wives without giving reason. The routine is one of speaking the words "I divorce you" three times, followed by notification to the religious and legal authorities.

Women, on the other hand, are under obligation to prove that the man is either impotent, or that he is not financially capable of supporting a wife and family. Or, if the man has more than one wife, a woman can try to make the case that he is not providing equally for all wives. Even then, the religious authorities generally side with the man, telling the woman to go home, that God knows best what is good for her.

I am thinking without speaking. It is painfully obvious that Nayam cannot claim that Obeid is impotent. He may well be the most potent man in the kingdom. Since she is his only wife and lives in obvious physical comfort, the second reason for woman-directed divorce is also invalid.

Nayam has a problem.

Her family either cannot, or will not, go against her husband.

Nayam recognizes clearly the ugly hopelessness of her personal circumstances. Tears continue to stream down her face.

I shift uncomfortably and ponder an appropriate response to my distraught visitor.

Her gentle face wrinkled in agony, Nayam suddenly pulls the veil over her eyes and abruptly stands. "Obeid will be looking for me. He will be furious that I ran away."

I lightly brush her arm with my outstretched hand. "Please, I want to know what happens with your baby...and with you." I plead with her, searching for words that will make an impact. "Nayam, I truly care. Please, come by my office any time you visit the hospital."

She stops and turns, a stranger swathed in black shroud once more, facing me, but without a face. "I can call you?" she questions hesitantly.

"Yes!" I move toward my desk and quickly write down my office phone number, my MCV apartment phone number, and the phone number at Peter's villa. I write my name, Jean Parks, at the top of the paper.

"John Park," she repeats in her beautiful accented voice.

I smile. "Jean Parks."

She does not offer me her phone number, but not for rudeness. Nayam would be afraid for Obeid to discover that we have ever met. Surely this is a man who would forbid his wife a friendship with an American woman.

I watch her small black-cloaked form as she seemingly floats up the hallway and to the elevator.

I am sure that I will never see or speak with the gentle Nayam again.

But I am wrong. Surprisingly, she calls several times over the course of the next few months.

As the years pass, I am to learn that telephone conversations create a comfort embraced by many Saudi women. Quite simply, many Saudi females readily reveal intimate secrets, even to strangers, during telephone conversations. I have heard of some young women, bolder than most, who dial random numbers, whispering sexual promises to men who answer, strangers to them.

The reason for this behavior is a mystery that I cannot solve. But it does seem that every human being living in bondage finds an outlet for secret pleasures.

Nayam speaks openly when she phones, telling me that her situation has not improved.

My heart pounds painfully when I hear that Shaker, her baby son, is still living a miserable life of cruel deformity.

Nayam suffers through several more pregnancies; all, she is pleased to report, ended in spontaneous miscarriages.

I do not know whether to be happy or sad for her lost pregnancies. Perhaps some of those children would have been without deformity, although considering the parents' genetic history, such a thing is doubtful. "And Obeid?" I ask. "Has he changed?"

"Nothing of Obeid will ever change," she replies in her sweet voice.

As I listen to Nayam speak, I remember my vow that I will persuade Saudi women to fight for their own freedom.

I believe that Nayam's unusual childhood, which had been grounded in thoughts of female self-determination, layered by a good education, will make her open to my ideas. I feel certain I have met the woman who can help bring important change to Saudi culture. But first she must be able to break away from her own oppression. With a sick child, constant pregnancies, and a demanding husband, will she have the energy for such a cause?

Too nervous to approach the topic in a straightforward manner, I read her a short poem I wrote.

"Nayam, listen. This is something special. Something for you," I tell her with a rush of excitement.

"This is about the Saudi tradition of cousins marrying cousins."

"A man's first cousin is not a proper wife.
The good doctors at the KFSH quote medical
    statistics,
warning unyielding hawk-nosed men that each
    child born
from a "cousin coupling" is in grave danger of a
    short-lived painful life.
I listen as Bedouin husbands argue that all is in
    Allah's capable hands.
These two resolute forces remind me of tenacious
    rivals taut with strife,
each determined to be triumphant, yet both
    destined to lose.

Meanwhile, wounded women are caught in this
    merciless web,
while innocent Arab babies burst into a cruel
    world,
their deformed bodies tormenting them,
as well as those who love them."

Nayam is quiet. She thanks me, saying, "I did not know American people are verse makers."

"We are not talented poets like you Saudis," I confess, "but I know many Americans who write a poem occasionally." I add, "I've been writing poems since I was a teenager." I speak words that I fear saying, even as they are spilling from my mouth. "Nayam, have you thought of forming a society for Saudi women?"

Her voice is high pitched when she says, "A society?"

"Yes. I'm speaking about a political organization where Saudi women can gather and make appeals to the government."

Her breathing becomes intense, but she does not respond.

Her silence encourages me.

"Perhaps a women's society that could present one important issue at the time, such as the issue of veils, and then the issue of divorce without cause, and then the issue of..."

"Jean. I beg you. Stop. Do you want me to languish in a dungeon? Who would take care of my son?"

"Well...with Western influence making an appearance in Saudi Arabia, don't you think that your government is moving forward on key issues relating to women?"

Her accent thickens. "*No. I do not.*" She begins to speak rapidly with a sudden coldness in her tone. "This is dangerous talk. I do not like it."

"I..."

"Shaker is crying. I must go."

A click of the phone and the call abruptly ends. I stand there holding the receiver in my hand, feeling rather foolish.

"Well, I could have handled that much better," I tell myself as I hang up the phone.

As I mull over our conversation, I realize that Nayam was right to be concerned. There is no patience for activist activities within the kingdom. There's no such thing as civilian protests in Saudi Arabia. People are not even allowed to gather in large crowds. There are no movie theaters, no bowling alleys, and very few independent organizations, since such groups must be licensed by the government. Even if a license is granted, the organization will be carefully monitored by the religious authorities. Even private groups that do nothing but read the Koran are often shut down.

In Saudi Arabia, any large gatherings, other than weddings, are forbidden by law.

Never again do I hear Nayam's sweet voice. Apparently Nayam believes her association with me is too dangerous. I'm wretchedly sad when I realize that I moved much too quickly with this Saudi woman. I've lost contact with a woman whom I truly cared about. I have learned a painful lesson.

But I'm not willing to abandon my efforts to change the fate of these veiled women. I realize that I must become clever with my techniques and encourage these women to reach conclusions *on their own*. I won't suggest the formation of organizations but 1 will try to lead them to reach that idea themselves.

But to make this happen, I must become friendly with other Saudi women. I want to meet them in their homes and get to know them. That's the only way they'll ever grow to trust me and what I have to say.

Chapter Eleven
Jeddah Chick Asma

A few weeks later, when I'm invited to a royal wedding at the invitation of a minor princess I met through Saudi friends, I eagerly accept. I've attended a few other Saudi weddings and I've found them to be over-the-top fun. I've enjoyed dressing up and spending time with so many interesting and beautiful Saudi women. But now I've got a more serious agenda.

Hotels in Saudi Arabia build special rooms to host Saudi wedding parties. Unlike Christian weddings and Jewish weddings, which are often held in places of worship, Muslim weddings are not conducted in mosques.

Mosques are for men to gather for prayer, for discussion of the Prophet's teachings, or for secret political meetings. While females are allowed inside the largest and most holy mosques in Mecca and Medina, and in particular during holy times of Ramadan and Haj, I've never known women to participate in events inside any of the numerous neighborhood mosques within the kingdom. In fact, women are discouraged from praying in local mosques.

Many times during the *muezzin's* call to prayer, I've gazed out on the street from the rooftop at Peter's villa watching the crowds of Saudi men spill from their homes to walk to the neighborhood mosque. No women walk beside them. Instead, I often watched as solitary Saudi women bowed to Mecca from the small balconies. Those who did not venture outside to their balconies, obviously prayed to Allah from the interior of their homes.

Weddings, too, are sexually segregated. On the occasion of this female-only celebration of an upcoming wedding I am the guest of Princess Selma, a minor princess in the House of al-Saud, meaning that the men in her family are not in line to the throne. Princess Selma and I became friendly a year ago. We met through mutual friends at a women's party, when one of the doctor's wives at the KFSH invited me to accompany her. Learning of my interest in her culture, Princess Selma had kindly invited me to several Saudi social functions since then.

Selma is in the backseat of a black Mercedes when her chauffeur arrives to pick me up in front of Peter's villa. She looks unusually attractive on this night. Although she was born with a prominent nose that curls over thin lips, Selma employs a skilled make-up artist from Morocco who diminishes her nose while plumping her lips. The result is strikingly flattering.

Selma's dress is a lovely pink silk gown with delicate pink pearls on the bodice. Diamond earrings are swinging from her ears and her neck is embraced by a band of emeralds and diamonds.

I'm wearing a multicolored silk blouse and matching long skirt that I recently purchased in Milan, Italy, when I traveled there with Peter to visit his parents. My hair is hanging long and straight down my back without any adornments[7].

Before we step out of the Mercedes, Selma throws a cloak and scarf over her dress. My attire is modest with arms and legs fully covered, so I step out without the usual black cloak and head scarf.

Selma's fingers brush through my hair as we walk into the large hall. "Allah blessed you with this hair," she says with a smile.

---

[7] For a photo of Jean dressed for the royal wedding, please visit http://jeansasson.com/books/american-chick-gallery.html

"What a sweet thing to say. Thank you," I reply, hugging her.

We enter the hotel arm in arm. This wedding is not as elaborate as previous weddings I've attended, but still it is a flamboyant affair. I smile in approval at the understated elegance of the decorations. For my taste, Saudi celebrations are often garish. But tonight the flowers are simple yellow carnations and white roses. The coverings on the tables and seats are yellow silk. Large white candles are centered on each table-top.

After removing her cloak and veil to hand them to an attendant, Selma takes my hand and leads me to a group of her friends who are talking and laughing, happy to be celebrating. Although every blonde-haired foreign female stirs wondrous curiosity in the kingdom, the lengthy fall of my hair always piques added fascination.

I am equally fascinated by the exotic Saudi women. With their glowing bronzed skin, raven hair, and chocolate eyes, most Saudi women are very attractive.

Each elaborate dress is stunning, and a few dazzling gowns are stitched with precious stones. Their dark hair is elaborately coifed and decorated with jeweled pins, and expensive jewelry drapes every neck and wrist.

I'm relieved that many of the women have a good command of English, which will make the evening more pleasant for me. Since Dr. Feteih frequently speaks with members of the royal family from our Medical Affairs offices, I've been asked not to learn Arabic, so to promote royal privacy. But these women do not know this, so I feel a quick flush of shame that I still do not speak their language.

Although everyone exclaims over my dress and hair with gushing compliments, I notice a few women glancing at my bare neck, wrists and fingers with a look of pity. Most upper-class Saudi women attach enormous importance to expensive gowns and costly jewels. It's one

84

of the ways they can express their individuality and their status.

Our group approaches overloaded tables stacked with gourmet food. I begin with a sample of some of the Beluga caviar and smoked salmon before accepting a glass of cold apple juice.

Since alcohol is banned in the kingdom, there is none visible at this female event. When more than one woman whispers to me that there is a store of alcohol in a small room adjoining the large wedding hall, I smile. I suppose they expect that all Western women drink alcohol.

When I was recruited by HCA, I was warned that if giving up alcohol would be a hardship for me, I should not accept the offered position. So I was surprised to learn that alcohol is readily available in the kingdom. Wealthy Saudis have access to anything they desire, including alcohol. And, most expatriates make it themselves or they buy it on the black market.

Suddenly the throb and crash of loud drums and cymbals fill the air. A group of female dancers mingles through the crowd. They are dressed in golden costumes, delighting the eye with their adroit moves. One of Selma's friends shouts that the women are from the Sudan and Egypt. The dancers make their living traveling to the wealthy Gulf nations to perform at female celebrations.

The mood is one of happy anticipation. Everyone is waiting to see the bride, who we hear is an educated girl from a professional family. She is marrying "up" in society, into the royal family, which is a triumphant occasion for her and for her family. A few of the women seem jealous of the bride's good fortune and make cruel remarks about her. "She is of the tents," I hear one say scornfully.

The outspoken woman becomes quiet after Selma gives her a fierce look.

Women of the royal family are always shown deference by non-royals. Anytime a member of the royal family approaches a group of women, the other women react with respect. Jewel-covered hands are often kissed, although Muslims believe that no man or woman is above another in the eyes of God.

Within the hour, a lovely girl in a Western-style white beaded wedding dress walks through the room. This bride is very pretty and appears extremely happy.

Selma whispers that the young woman is marrying one of Selma's cousins and that the young man is known for his gentle manner.

I think of the soft-spoken Obeid and hope that this groom is not another man of deception. After the wedding, the groom will be free to do as he pleases, knowing that there is no authority that cares one whit about his wife's happiness.

The groom soon enters the hall, one of only six men in attendance. He goes to his bride like a man in a trance and doesn't seem to notice the mass of unveiled women staring intently at him. I exchange smiles with Selma. The groom's behavior is a hopeful beginning, I tell myself, recalling a wedding where the groom shocked all by ogling his wife's friends.

After bride and groom are presented and congratulated by those present, the event breaks into small groups. Some women return to the food while others begin to dance with female partners. I openly stare. It's routine for females to partner with females at Saudi weddings, but the sight of women dancing suggestively for each other is a scene I've never grown accustomed to seeing.

When a beautiful Saudi woman glides toward me, takes my hand in hers, and pulls me to the dance floor, I recoil awkwardly. I've never danced with another woman. I know it will be a serious affront to this woman if I balk at her invitation. I glance at Selma in the hope she will intervene, but she is busy talking and gesturing to two women at once. There's nothing to do but move to the beat of the music.

My dance partner tries to make conversation over the sounds of the loud music. But her words are in Arabic, so I respond with a smile and a shrug. I continue dancing, dearly longing to remove myself from the dance floor.

"Lord. Mama would die," I mumble to myself even as I maintain a brave face.

I grew up in one of the most conservative regions of America's Bible Belt and any type of dancing is considered slightly sinful. The Saudi custom of women dancing with women would thoroughly shock all the people I know and love in my small hometown.

I'm searching the crowd, looking for rescue, when my partner reaches over and tries to pull me close. This woman is taller than me. I look up and am astonished to see that her lips are beginning to pucker!

I involuntarily shout, "No, no," and place my hand over my mouth.

My dancing partner freezes in place.

Suddenly strong hands pull me backward and off the dance floor.

Another beautiful Saudi woman has me in her hands. Believing I am in some kind of danger, I begin to struggle.

Selma runs to me and begins to sputter in anger, "She is my guest!"

The woman who saves me begins to laugh. "Your guest was about to receive one of Latifa's special kisses! I saved her."

By this time several chattering women encircle us.

"If I were married to Latifa's husband, I would kiss women, too," one says with a hearty laugh. "He's a most unattractive man with a stomach this big," she mutters as she circles her hands in a rounded gesture across her midsection.

An older Saudi woman glares in Latifa's direction. "That woman is strong. My daughter Sara told me the force of Latifa's kiss sucked her tongue straight through her lips and into Latifa's mouth!"

"Latifa is too wild," Selma mutters while glancing over my shoulder and at the dance floor. She looks back at me. "Jean, never mind Latifa. She tries to kiss all the new girls. She means no harm."

I turn back to look at Latifa. She is staring at me with an expression of disappointment. For the first time I notice Latifa's athletic body. She is a large woman with muscles.

I shiver at the thought of my narrow escape.

My thoughts are interrupted with an introduction from one of the most beautiful women I've ever seen. "I am Asma."

I instantly recognize her as the woman who pulled me from Latifa's arms. Before I have an opportunity to thank her, Asma's sister and five other women quickly join us. Saying that they have been watching my long blonde hair swing while on the dance floor, all their attention is focused on me.

When these women discover that not only am I unmarried, but that I have traveled around the world as a single female to live and work in a royal hospital in their country, they are intrigued.

Hand in hand, we saunter over to a large table with chairs and seat ourselves where a lively conversation develops.

I detect a mixture of emotions as hurried questions come from every corner. Two of the women even clutch at my arms and express their horror that I am a woman who works to provide for myself and to support my parents. Such a financial burden is beyond their comprehension.

"If you do not work, does that mean you do not eat?" Asma inquires with a steady gaze.

"Well, I suppose that is right." I laugh heartily. "I've been feeding myself for most of my adult life, and guess what?" I circle my waist, which has increased by a few inches since I first arrived in the kingdom, with my hands and exclaim. "I've missed no meals!"

No one laughs. Several women exchange alarmed looks and Asma shakes her head in sorrow and says, "Oh, Allah! She would not have a piece of bread if she did not labor!"

Asma's sister voiced what seemed to be an unspoken, yet unanimous opinion. "When I hear such stories, I feel blessed to be a Saudi woman. Pass me my veil! I am happy to wear it, now."

Several women giggle while others mumble their heartfelt full agreement.

I am assuredly the one to be pitied in their eyes.

By the end of the wedding, I have not inspired anyone to reject the Saudi status quo. But I have received a number of heartfelt invitations to individual Saudi homes. I smile, thinking that these sweet women are concerned that I will not have enough to eat. They want to take care of me, just as I want to take care of them.

Months later when I receive a coveted invitation to spend a few days at Asma's palace in Jeddah, I am elated—even though Asma makes it clear that she's most eager to share her highly developed methods in "catching and keeping a man." In Asma's mind, a thirty-three-year-old unmarried female is a challenge to be met!

Asma simply does not believe me when I tell her that marriage and motherhood are not my goals in life. Besides, I have been married twice. Although married to fine men whom I once loved, and still respect, I found myself bored and restless.

Despite her great beauty and endless talk about pleasing her husband, Asma does have a serious and thoughtful side to her. Sitting alone and talking, she is surprisingly relaxed and open, seemingly willing to talk about any subject. Perhaps that is because none of her Saudi friends are around, ready to judge. I know from my short time in the kingdom that all Saudis worry over Saudi opinion. All Saudis I have met act more relaxed around Westerners.

Asma readily answers my questions about her education at a prestigious girl's school in Switzerland.

I am sorry to learn that Asma chose to stop her schooling and return to Saudi Arabia to get married.

"Europe made me uncomfortably free," Asma confesses with a flippant air.

Her answer is so unexpected that my own voice rises sharply with surprise at her astounding revelation. "You are uncomfortable with freedom?"

"You asked how I could leave Europe and return to a life behind the veil? Well, I am telling you."

"Are you telling me that freedom was the problem?" My eyes narrowed. "Asma, there are people all over our world who die for freedom."

With a faraway look in her eyes, Asma whispers, "Your freedom is not my freedom." She leans closer to me. "Jean, do you know that women in Europe become intimate with men on the first night of their meeting?"

I clamp my teeth together before admitting, "Well. Some women, Asma. Not all."

Asma makes a clicking sound, meaning "no," with her tongue. "No. You are wrong. Most Western women act like men. I knew seven girls very well at my boarding school. Six of the seven thought sex was a joke. As we got ready to go out at night these women would take bets about who would get into bed with a man the fastest!"

I nod. The sexual revolution of the 1960s had definitely spread around the globe. Yet, I so want to convince this bright woman that freedom should be her goal. "Listen, please. In the West, females are free to make mistakes. Then they must try to sift through the problems created by that mistake. That is the beauty of a normal life. Ordinary people make mistakes. Ordinary people learn from those mistakes and hopefully do better the next time around."

I watch for a moment, thinking.

Asma makes a rumbling sound in her throat before speaking with arrogant certainty. "Such mistakes do not make an honorable life for a virtuous woman. My great-grandfather was a proud Bedouin. He would not rest in paradise if his great-granddaughter was polluted in that atmosphere."

I watch quietly as she fusses with her hair. "So, I told my father that for the sake of family honor, I wanted to come back to Saudi Arabia. I wished to have an early marriage."

I am searching for a convincing argument. "Well, Asma, no one could force you to take up bad habits. I knew plenty of women in college who drank alcohol and smoked cigarettes, but I knew many others who did not. In Europe, you were free to say no." I lean forward to emphasize my point. "It's all about freedom. The freedom to do right, or to do wrong. Personal freedom."

She twists the largest of three enormous diamond rings around her finger and then speaks again. "I felt unclean around those women."

I pick up my soda and spin the ice cubes with my finger, giving myself time to form the perfect response. "Asma, Saudi women must change their own lives. There is little that others can do for you. Wealthy and educated women can be the salvation for every Saudi woman. Very few Saudi women have the opportunity to travel to another country, acquire an education, and experience complete freedom. You should have taken that chance to prove to everyone that you could make the most of freedom without sinking to the immoral depths that freedom allows." I grimace as I shrug my shoulders. "Here you are so confined."

"My heart is not confined!"

"You are confined in many ways, Asma."

The true misery of my own experience under the veil hovers nearby, but I say nothing for fear my story will be misinterpreted. I know firsthand what it felt to walk veiled in the hot desert sun and to bake under the black cloak. I know with certainty that many women in the kingdom have no say-so over who they will marry. I know that there are many miserable women in the kingdom, and that their misery could be relieved by a good dose of freedom to make their own decisions.

Her voice is firm. "Despite the troubles for women in my country, I wanted to live a Saudi life. I prefer my life to the life of a European woman." She smiles. "Saudi life is best for Saudi women."

I sigh deeply, thinking that my efforts have been futile once again. I sadly reflect on the lives of wealthy Saudi women. From my personal experiences, it is evident that so many wealthy females within the kingdom are devoted to little else but frivolity, with their thoughts focused mainly on their looks and their luxurious possessions.

I study Asma's face and figure. She stands framed against the beauty of a priceless tapestry as she justifies her life behind the veil.

My Saudi friend meets every standard of beauty, Eastern or Western. Her hair is a mesh of rich raven and her skin is bright and clear. Her face is Arab perfection. Her chocolate eyes are large and full. Her nose is defining without dominating. Her mouth is small, but her lips are full and colorful. Her neck is smooth. Her shoulders are broad. Her figure is buxom, but her long legs counter her full figure. Her hands are baby-soft and graced with long fingers adorned in costly jewelry.

Asma is a perfect vision of beauty. I had heard gossip about the benefits of her beauty at a women's party. Asma, I was told, enjoyed more offers of marriage than all of her five full sisters and eleven half sisters combined.

Two years ago, she married an exceptionally wealthy and powerful Saudi executive involved in the oil industry. Not surprising, her husband is a third cousin on her mother's side of the family.

Again and again I have been told by Saudi men and women that a marriage between cousins is a clever idea. Such a marriage, so the thinking goes, enriches one's extended family rather than weakening it.

I wonder if Saudis will ever change their thinking on this incredibly incorrect idea. Accustomed for generations to living by rigid tradition, they often have great difficulty accepting scientific facts.

I've been told that Asma's husband, Khalid, is one of the wealthiest non-royals in the kingdom. He is more than twenty years her senior, but she tells me that she feels treasured by the wisdom of an older husband. She is extremely proud to be his only wife.

I inwardly wince as Asma complacently announces, "I follow my husband's advice on every important matter."

Asma's full lips are now pulsing with words of certainty. "I am proud to be a Saudi woman. I dislike it when people from the West discuss our lives and talk about our misery, even as they admit they have never met a Saudi woman!" She fingers the circlet of diamonds around her neck before tugging at the luscious gown wrapped loosely about her form. "And I believe that my veil protects me."

A smile breaks over my face. "Oh?"

I had heard Saudi women offer this argument many times over the past few years. To my profound bewilderment, many are convinced that the restrictive veil and numerous social restrictions protect them.

93

Asma relishes drama, and now her voice climbs as she counts off the arguments for her controlled Saudi life on her fingers.

"We have the best society for women. God had the perfect plan for men and women. Men are strong and women are weak. Men have their role as protectors. Women have their role as nurturers."

She snaps her fingers, eager to convert me to her way of thinking. "God made men and women so that every part of both will fit. The man's chest and belly is flat so it will not crush a woman's full chest. The male organ is a perfect match for the woman's secret place. The skin of a man is too strong to stretch and make room for babies, unlike the flexible skin of a female. After an infant is welcomed to this earth, someone must take care for it. Are men suitable for such work? No. It is a woman's job."

She pauses for a moment.

"Girls are now educated, but God put a special internal ingredient in a woman's center. Our hearts pull us to our families. If I could not see my infant daughter every day, I would shrivel like a desert flower in the noonday sun."

With those dramatic words, Asma's body twirls in a circle then crumples as she portrays the look of a wilting flower.

I burst out laughing. Asma is as convincing and talented as a trained actress.

She pulls herself up, her lips forming into a sexy pout. "Jean, women are happiest at home."

I take another sip of my soda before teasing her. "Okay. Okay. You've converted me! I'll buy the thickest and heaviest veil the next time I go shopping in Riyadh. Perhaps I'll become the fourth wife of a wealthy sheik."

A frown crosses Asma's face as she drops down on the dark-blue silk sofa. She knows that I am not seeking to marry any Saudi man. She does not appreciate my attempt at humor. "Do not tease me, Jean." With a dominating personality backed by wealth, she is accustomed to obedience from those females around her. She takes a few deep breaths, waiting for me to bridge the small gap in our conversation.

Asma is disarmingly childlike when she sulks.

I resume the conversation. "Asma, we are from totally different worlds. Of course we see women's roles in our own way." I think for a minute then say, "People always defend what they know."

She quickly revisits the theme of my visit. "Once you learn how to *get* a man and how to *keep* a man, your thinking will change!"

I can barely contain my merriment at Asma's total focus on the subject of men.

She playfully tosses a small square pillow at me.

I throw it back and she yelps. Her vitality and high spirits instantly return.

When I first arrived in Saudi Arabia, I concluded that a society where women were veiled, guarded, and controlled by men would produce females uninterested in sex. I was wrong. Nearly every Saudi woman I know is passionately preoccupied with the three important topics of men, sex, and marriage.

At every Saudi female function, men, marriage, and motherhood follow fashion as the prime focus of conversation. If a woman is *not* married, the dialogue centers around single men considered good catches. If the woman *is* married, the exchange revolves around birthing and babies and the importance of sons. If the woman happens to be of a certain age, the conversation focuses on her marriageable sons and grandsons.

I have never known women more obsessed with every detail involving relationships with the opposite sex.

Since I have been in the kingdom for several years and remain unmarried, Asma is committed to the idea that I am a failure as a woman. The fact that Peter Sasson and I had a rare and serious argument the week before has excited her. The following day he traveled out of the kingdom to Europe. In Asma's opinion, the argument was just cause for a crash course in how to catch a new man.

Asma insists that she will be my instructor, often hinting that she has perfected the art of keeping a man's interest.

Asma claims, "I keep Khalid so contented that no other woman comes to his mind." She proudly announces, "Not even in his sleep!"

Admittedly, I am bewildered at the concept of anyone teaching a southern American woman ploys for ensnaring men. Women from America's Deep South are well-known for their feminine wiles. But out of curiosity, I am eager to hear Asma's wisdoms.

I lurch in alarm when Asma leaps from the sofa and squeals.

"What?" I ask.

"Khalid will be home soon!" She dashes from the room. "I must prepare myself!"

I am baffled. Already Asma is an image of feminine perfection. What else could she possibly do to prepare for her husband's arrival?

"Tonight I will give you your first lesson," she shouts as she passes through an open doorway.

I cannot restrain my delight at Asma's childlike excitement.

Asma, like many Saudi women, is a study in contrasts. She is a relatively well-educated woman who can discuss international events. Yet she can, and often does, lapse into childlike dramatics. She will weep when hearing a sad story, yet she can be unkind to her own servants.

While waiting, I stroll through the living quarters of Asma's palace, which glitters with priceless furnishings. Each room reaches up to a towering ceiling and is filled with over-size furniture. The sitting room alone can easily accommodate a hundred guests.

I have been a guest in several royal palaces. In what often seems a stiff competition, each new Saudi palace is designed and furnished to be more extravagant than those already built. Bathroom and kitchen fixtures are fashioned out of gold. Exquisite furniture imported from Italy adorns immense rooms. Sofas are cushioned with silk fabrics. Priceless carpets soften every step. Brilliant chandeliers hang overhead.

At meals and parties, banquet tables are laden with fish, fowl, fruit, and rare delicacies. Flowered centerpieces are flown in from the East. The desert air is scented with heavy perfumes. Every surface is lovely and shimmers with golden tones.

Asma's pink palace is perched on the shoreline of the Red Sea. Earlier she announced that several royals are neighbors. When I glance out the floor-to-ceiling windows, I can see that Asma's small garden is dotted with blooming flowers and swaying palm trees. I am in a desert kingdom but I could be in sultry Hawaii.

I wait in the windowed sitting room for Asma to make her grand entrance.

An hour later Asma glides dramatically through the doorway. Her beauty is so exquisite that she could and should forgo cosmetic assistance. But her makeup is heavily applied. Her dark-lidded eyes bring to mind the beauty of Elizabeth Taylor in the movie *Cleopatra*. Her black hair is pulled back on one side and adorned with a jeweled rose. A ruby-and-diamond necklace matches her ruby earrings and two diamond bracelets. She has replaced three diamond rings with two of the largest ruby rings I've ever seen.

Although she is a mentally bright woman, Asma clearly uses her beauty rather than her mind as the instrument to keep her husband happy.

From what I have learned in life, the opposite approach is more often successful. While most men are first drawn to physical beauty, such an attraction does not last without a more engaging peg on which a man can hang his hat, or in this case, his *ghutrah.*

I nod in admiration. "You look gorgeous."

Her red lips curve in satisfaction. "You will learn good lessons tonight, Jean." She places her hands on her hips. "I am the best teacher. I will teach you how to get a man and how to keep a man."

I suppress my smile. "All right, then."

"Do you like this dress? A French designer made only one. For me."

"It's extraordinary," I truthfully tell her.

Asma's scoop-necked ball gown is a burst of red. The costly dress rises to her knees in the front, cascades longer in the back, and terminates in a ruffled train that flows behind. When she uses her hands to lift her breasts into shocking prominence, I see that her perfectly manicured fingernails match the color of her red lips.

"Khalid loves this dress," she assures me. "He likes me to tease him with my breasts." She laughs. "Of course, I can only wear such a dress if there are no other men present." She tightens her lips and emphasizes with her index finger. "My Khalid is *very* jealous, you know."

"Yes, you told me."

"He likes for me to be tall, as well," she explains, atop three-inch high-heeled gold shoes that raise her five-seven height to a tall woman of five-ten.

I sigh. This Saudi beauty will tower over my five-two form. High heels hurt my feet. I'd given them up a few years back.

The door opens and Khalid appears.

I'm instantly disappointed. Khalid has small brown eyes, a sharp nose, plump cheeks, and a double chin. He's shorter than his wife, who jolts me with her high-pitched greeting.

"*Khalid!*"

I've never seen a woman rush toward a man with such enthusiasm. The scene reminds me of a rodeo rider rushing to the prize steer.

Khalid appears taken aback by his wife's energetic greeting. Light of foot, he nimbly takes a few steps backwards.

She gushes, "Khalid, my husband, I have given strict orders to the servants. No hands but mine will care for you on this night."

With that, she jerks Khalid's cloth headdress (*ghutrah*) and the black cord that holds it down (*agal*) off his head.

The poor man covers his baldness with his *ghutrah* and now looks momentarily embarrassed in front of a stranger.

While waving his headdress, she gaily asks, "What does my strong protector wish to drink?"

Towering over her husband, she gives me a knowing look, winking and smiling.

Using the lure of her beautiful face and lush body, Asma then swings her body around and in front of her husband, ensuring that he can easily see her cleavage.

With a lift of his brows, Khalid looks away.

She's wasting those huge breasts, I think to myself.

"Ah, Khalid, where are my manners? This is my American friend. The Jean I told you about."

I stand up. I smile.

With a slight frown, Khalid looks at me and nods. "You are most welcome to my home, Jean."

"Thank you, Khalid. Your home is very beautiful."

The edge of his lips rises into a faint smile.

I sense that Khalid is not thrilled to discover a house guest. But there is nothing to be done but to make the best of it, so I settle comfortably on the sofa, remaining a quiet observer of the evening.

Asma rushes to the bar and begins to place ice cubes in a glass. "Do you want your usual? A scotch and soda?"

"Yes, that is good, Asma," Khalid replies wearily.

"Jean?" Asma asks, "What would you like to drink?"

Not wanting to interrupt her full attention away from Khalid, I refuse her offer. "Thank you, Asma. Something later, perhaps."

Asma presents Khalid with his drink without comment before unexpectedly reaching down to the floor.

I am so startled that I glance to see what is going on.

Asma is tugging determinedly at Khalid's sandals.

Generally Saudis remove their shoes before entering their homes, but Khalid has not done so, for whatever the reason.

"Asma? What are you doing?" the bewildered man asks.

"I want to make my husband happy, Khalid," Asma smilingly replies. "Your feet are surely tired after a long day. I will rub them for you. That will make you happy."

While Asma's beauty redeems a multiple of faults, she is reaching her limit with Khalid. He pulls his wife's hands away from his feet. His voice is edged with irritation. "I *will* be happy if you sit, Asma. Sit and talk with us."

"After I get your favorite snack." Asma stretches to pick up a servant's summoning bell and gives it an enthusiastic ring. Two small Indonesian women must have been waiting by the door, for they make an abrupt appearance. One is balancing a golden tray laden with expensive beluga caviar. The other maid is carrying a tray holding all the usual condiments.

"Khalid's preferred food," Asma explains with a broad smile. "I order it by the pound from a special supplier in Switzerland." She rubs Khalid's shoulder before preparing a small plate filled with caviar and then insists that Khalid listen to a short poem she has composed in his honor.

"You can save the poem for later, if you like," the increasingly polite Khalid suggests in a low voice.

"No! No! Jean must hear this. I insist!"

She clears her voice. Just as Asma begins to speak, her pet cat comes running into the room and jumps into his mistress' lap.

Asma's face contorts with her shrill words.

"Oh Khalid! Oh Khalid! Oh Khalid!
See my lips, how red they are!
Oh Khalid! Oh Khalid! Oh Khalid!
I am blessed by your love!
Oh Khalid! Oh Khalid! Oh..."

Asma's cat begins to meow loudly.

To my ear, the cat's cries are in perfect rhythm with Asma's words and voice. Dear God, I tell myself, even the cat is beginning to meow in verse. I'm so embarrassed that my cheeks flush.

As Asma's voice grows louder in tandem with the cat's noisy meows, Khalid jumps to his feet. "Asma. Enough! Thank you. That was very special."

The evening deteriorates from that point. After an awkward dinner during which Asma attempts to hand-feed the tense Khalid, she insists upon a game of backgammon.

I know that Asma is a champion backgammon player, but she allows Khalid to win every game.

I play a few games but am not skilled enough to win. To my mind, Khalid is a man who desperately needs a feminine challenge, someone who will defeat him at parlor games and match him in intelligence.

As the evening stretches on, I become exasperated while viewing the energy Asma expends to entertain her husband.

Khalid is wearing a suffering look of boredom tinged with annoyance.

I imagine that I see a line of bitterness growing from Khalid's nose down to the corners of his mouth.

When the frazzled man retires for the evening, Asma walks him to the door with promises of joining him soon. She teases him with whispered words that I am unable to hear.

With Khalid out of earshot, Asma turns happily toward me. "Jean, see how happy I make my husband?"

I am speechless.

"Well, did you learn anything?"

"I did, Asma. Yes. I did," I answer mildly.

"Well, now you know. That's how you *get* a man, and that's how you *keep* a man."

I think better of sharing my opinion and say nothing.

Unsurprisingly, Khalid departs the following morning before Asma wakes. He leaves a message with the servants that he has been summoned to Spain by one of the royals to attend an emergency meeting.

Oh, my! He's fled the country, I think to myself. This is not good.

The next morning a happy Asma waves good-bye, convinced she has presented me with skillful lessons that will change my life. For the next few months she calls me frequently to see if I have yet to implement her techniques for husband catching. Asma is sweet-natured and genuinely concerned about my single state. Although I do not agree with her tactics, I know I am lucky to have such a concerned friend.

Then one morning I hear from a highly agitated Asma.

Her voice thick with anger, she shouts, "May Khalid be boiled in oil!"

"Asma? What?"

"Khalid is taking a second wife!"

"Oh, no!"

"He said I cackle like a hen all day!"

"Well...I..."

"He insults me! He claims I cackle so loud he looks to see me lay an egg!"

"What brought..."

Her voice is so shrill that I hold the phone receiver away from my ear. "Khalid says my voice is so noisy that his mother can hear me in her house! Jean! His mother lives in *Taif*!"

"When did this happen?"

Her proud temper is shining. "God is counting my tears!"

"What..."

"Khalid will suffer at God's hands for every tear!"

Her voice breaks, "I wish I could cause his death with one glance!"

"Asma, listen..."

She heaves a sob before threatening, "Tonight while he sleeps, I will tear out his eyes with thorns!"

Trying to turn her emotions, I steer her into logical thought. "What will you do?"

Painful sobs rend the air. "I give him my beauty and he declines!"

I repeat, "What will you do?"

"What can I do?"

"Tell him no, that you will not accept a second wife."

"He can do what he pleases. He is a man!"

Knowing this is not the best time to bring up our earlier conversation about the lack of female power and personal freedom, I say nothing of what I really feel. I have learned during my time in the kingdom that the one

103

fear that nearly every Saudi woman shares is the terror that their husband will come home with another wife. The possibility of the second wife keeps most Saudi women insincerely obedient.

I want her to be resolute. "Well. You should divorce him. You are a wealthy woman in your own right. You are very smart. You can own a business or find a job. *Show him* that you are capable of a full life without him."

"I cannot." Her voice drops. "He might take my daughter." Her buoyant spirit suddenly shrank from the contemplation of future suffering. "For another woman to raise? I could not bear it."

"Perhaps not. Ask him."

I know that some educated Muslim men do not always press the issue of custody when the child in question is female.

"Perhaps Khalid will allow you to keep your only daughter."

"Never would he agree!"

"Who is he to marry?"

Her silence hung like a dreaded cleaver. Finally she admits the painful truth. "My cousin. Khalid is going to marry my young cousin. She is only eighteen years of age."

"Oh, my."

"This girl is like a sparrow, never saying a word! I am a songbird! Why would my husband want a sparrow when he has a songbird?"

Never could I speak the truthful words that would so wound my friend.

Finally her sobs become so loud that she is unable to continue the conversation.

I feel so sad. Although I want Asma to make an effort to get custody of her child and file for divorce, I know that Asma will bow to the infallibility of Saudi tradition. She will accept this indignity to her life. The joyous Asma will probably never again know the happiness and pleasure that her naïve nature provided her.

I sit alone with my thoughts for a long time, wondering what possible advice I can offer Asma.

My thoughts turn to Nayam, who is intelligent and educated. Nayam built her hopes around the idea of working in her chosen career.

But her husband said no.

Nayam would have welcomed another wife into her home to carry the burden of mothering her husband's children.

But her husband said no.

Now Nayam will continue having babies until she is beyond the age of childbirth, because her husband says she will.

I then consider the plight of Asma, who is beautiful and wealthy and too accommodating for her own good. Asma has shaped her entire life around the theme of pleasing her husband. Her grasping personality ensured failure. With the collapse of her well-thought out plan, she will exist in a special kind of agony.

Born to live in a land where men rule, neither woman had any control over their own destinies. The right to make important personal choices belongs to their husbands alone.

As the light of the sun turns into the dark of night, I have to confess to myself that I have done nothing fruitful for either Nayam or Asma. I cannot even convince them to help themselves. In Saudi Arabia, the power of men and expectations of culture combined are so daunting that only the bravest of women can find the courage to push for personal freedom.

I realize once more that I have been foolish to believe that I could bring change to the lives of Saudi women. The only certainty I can hold on to is this: When one sex is in total charge of the other, nothing turns out well. Not love, not marriage, not child-rearing, not business, not friendship. In a world where there is no equality between the genders, there is no hope for the future.

This is the hard lesson that I will learn over and over again for the next thirty years. Many exciting journeys will take me to Lebanon, to Bahrain, to Dubai, to Kuwait, to Iraq, to Thailand, and to many other countries. Ultimately I will befriend women who are unafraid to look the truth of their lives in the face, and who will take actions to improve their lives and help other women. I will befriend other women who are courageous and determined. These are the brave women who will become the subjects of my books.

Meanwhile, on this particular night in Riyadh, I prepare for bed. In the distance I can hear the sounds of Riyadh life, the call to prayer, the bustling traffic. My boyfriend, Peter, is at his villa. Tomorrow he will go to work while I will go to my office. We will grow closer in our relationship until we speak of marriage. And I will continue my watchful stance and try to make sense of a complicated country that I have grown to love, a country I now call my home.[8]

---

[8] For photos of Jean in Riyadh, please visit
http://jeansasson.com/books/american-chick-gallery.html

Appendix A
Update on Life for Women in Saudi Arabia

It's been thirty-three years since I first traveled to live in Saudi Arabia. Most Saudi women believed that great change would come to the kingdom during the three decades that have passed. This has not happened. Yes, there has been progress, but not *enough* progress.

Now it is 2012. With each passing year, we can only hope that this will be the year that Saudi women will be given the right to drive, to choose the veil or spurn it, to exercise assent in the selection of their own husbands, and to be able to work freely in their chosen professions.

The good news is that the year 2011 saw new rumblings for change. The bad news is that many Saudi men in positions of power remain resistant to true gains for women in the kingdom.

The good news is that the majority of Saudi women are graduating from high school and many are graduating from college. The bad news is that, although armed with a good education, few Saudi women find employment because social restrictions ban men and women from working together.

In 2012, Saudi females still face severe punishment for any perceived instance of moral misconduct. This punishment is meted out by the men of her family, and no one would dare question a man about the power he wields over his women. But, on a positive note, many Saudi men are seeing the light when it comes to rights for women. Privately they complain about the restrictions still in force against their wives and daughters. Publicly they remain too leery of repercussions to take their complaints to authorities. This reluctance must change, for until men move forward, it is impossible for women alone to gain ground.

In 2012, most Saudi women still cover their faces with the full veil. The positive news is that some women in Jeddah are tossing aside the face veil. In the characteristic black cloak and scarf, these Jeddah women maintain their Islamic modesty.

In 2012, women are still forbidden to drive, although the push for women to drive is growing. It is rumored that King Abdullah will soon make a positive decision on this important issue.

In 2012, girls are still forbidden to date and are often forced into arranged marriages. Young women are still given in marriage to old men. Once again, there is good news, for many fathers are backing away from committing their pre-teen daughters to marriage to men much too old for such a union.

In 2012, should a man choose to marry as many as four wives, his first wife can do nothing to stop him. The good news is that most educated men are content with one wife.

In 2012, wives cannot stop their husbands from divorcing them, even if there is *no* good cause. Yet wives still have difficulty divorcing their husbands, even if they *have* good cause.

In 2012, women have no one to save them should their fathers or husbands or brothers or even sons confine them to their homes.

In 2012, females are allowed a college education *only* if their father gives their permission. Females are still limited to certain professions that do not mix with the opposite sex. Females are not allowed to work with or near men who are not of their family. Despite the fact that most Saudi women are educated, only twelve percent of the Saudi workforce is female.

In 2012, females are still forbidden from traveling unless they have written permission from a male family member. The good news is that women are now allowed their own passport, rather than being restricted to a listing on their husband's passport. However, the bad news is that the men of the family generally keep the women's passports under their possession.

In 2012, mothers cannot even protest if their husbands murder their daughters in the name of honor killing.

In 2011, King Abdullah al-Saud decreed that women will be allowed to vote in the 2015 elections. The hope is that the men who control these women will drive them to the polls and allow them to vote. Despite the ruling that women can vote, without the permission of her husband, she will not vote.

In 2011, Crown Prince Sultan al-Saud died of cancer. Sultan's full brother, Prince Naif al-Saud moved into the position of Crown Prince. Prince Naif was well-known as one of the most radical of all the royal brothers, and women in the kingdom nervously voiced concern at the possible new restrictions they might face when Naif became king. But at age 78, Prince Naif had become increasingly unhealthy, and he too, died only eight months after being named as the heir apparent. At this time, his full brother, Prince Salman, was named the new Crown Prince. Prince Salman is one of the more popular princes and known to be more moderate than most. Saudi females are hopeful that Prince Salman will realize the importance of increasing rights for women in the kingdom, and will follow the lead of the current King Abdullah, who has introduced many needed reforms, and most particularly when it comes to the rights of women.

This author knowledgeably states that King Abdullah is one of the most popular kings to rule Saudi Arabia, and has been surprisingly supportive of women's rights. Although in many ways time has stood still for the women of Arabia, under King Abdullah there is slow change and renewed optimism. And as political movements continue to reshape expectations in many countries across the Middle East my hope grows that despite the men who rule them, the women of Saudi Arabia will soon gain freedoms for which they have yearned since the beginning of Arabian history.

I live for the happy day on which Saudi women can exercise the right to make their own decisions.

This has been a dream of mine since September 7, 1978.

Appendix B
About the Author and the American Chick Series

In 1978 I traveled abroad to Riyadh, Saudi Arabia, with a plan to live in that country for two years. I so greatly enjoyed my time in the desert kingdom that I remained there for twelve years. So much was happening in the Middle East during those twelve years that I personally experienced many exciting times, stories I will write when I expand this book.

The stories you have just read in *American Chick in Saudi Arabia* are true stories about real Saudi women. Here is an update on the women.

Although I returned to the Bedouin souk more than once, hoping to see Malaak, I was unsuccessful. I never again saw Malaak, the feisty Bedouin woman who so loved the life she was living. I'm convinced that she never experienced one moment of doubt that she was a lucky woman who had lived a wonderful life. For that I am glad.

I never again heard from Nayam, although when I told her story to Dr. Feteih, he was kind enough to use his position as head of the hospital to call for her medical records so that we might discover her history. I was devastated to learn that after giving birth to three more handicapped children, Nayam was diagnosed with cervical cancer and passed away one year later at the hospital. I had no way of finding out what happened to her greatly beloved "left behind" children, all who were battling serious medical issues.

Asma and I spoke several times after her husband married her cousin. Asma never had any other children with Khalid and found herself divorced one morning after learning that Khalid had married for a third time. Thankfully, Khalid allowed Asma to keep her daughter to raise until she turned thirteen, at which time he took his daughter to live in his household. Fortunately, he did allow Asma generous visitation rights, which amounted to an unusual victory in Saudi Arabia. Asma was such a sweet beauty that even after being divorced, she had a number of offers to marry wealthy and influential men. The last time we spoke, Asma was considering three different offers of marriage. She also decided to continue her education.

After residing in Saudi Arabia for five years I met a Saudi princess who fulfilled my dream of meeting a Saudi woman who was willing to fight for change. I told her life story in the international bestsellers, *Princess, Princess Sultana's Daughters* and *Princess Sultana's Circle.* The princess and I lived through other exciting adventures not revealed in the books about her life. With her assistance, I once disguised myself as a man to go undercover in Bangkok, Thailand, where I witnessed an auction of young girls into sex slavery, some of whom were likely taken back to Saudi Arabia. The princess and I wanted to know everything possible about that evil practice, hoping that somehow we might play a role in stopping the sex-slave trade into her country. To our immense sorrow, we were unsuccessful.

I was still living in Saudi Arabia when Osama bin Laden returned from the Soviet war in Afghanistan war to a hero's welcome. The reactions of Saudis left no doubt that Osama bin Laden was greatly loved and highly respected by most Saudi citizens. Little could the Saudis know that one day he would be a name well-known by nearly everyone on the planet. And I could have never guessed that I would one day be the biographer for Osama's first wife, the lovely and sweet Najwa, and their fourth-born son, the very brave and honorable Omar.

Najwa was a young wife and Omar a small child during the years I was a young woman happily living in their country.

I had many adventures with my husband Peter, an international man of great flair who also spoke a number of languages fluently. Since Peter had been born and raised to age eight in Alexandria, Egypt, he and I traveled to the country of his birth on many occasions. As a frequent visitor to Egypt, I came to know and love the Egyptian people, as well as the bustling city of Cairo and the tranquil city of Alexandria. Over the years I became aware of the radical religious movements sweeping that nation, often wondering where those movements would take Egypt. Now I know the answer to that question. Egypt has helped to lead the surprising Arab Spring, an entire region's determined quest for freedom.

Although Peter and I separated, and later divorced, we remained exceptionally close friends. I left Saudi Arabia but continued my world travels, for the travel bug had bitten. How could I have guessed that after twelve years of high excitement as a resident of ultra-conservative, yet exotic country of Saudi Arabia, I had not yet lived the most dramatic moments of my life?

From Saudi Arabia I traveled into Beirut during a time in which travel to Lebanon was forbidden for Americans. Kindly Lebanese customs officials agreed not to stamp my passport so that I might enter their beautiful country without repercussions from my own. My intense experiences in that country included visits to orphanages, where I met children who had lost entire families to the Lebanese civil war, visits to hospitals where critically wounded men and women lay wounded with little hope, and a searing visit to the Palestinian Shatila refugee camp where I met an elderly Palestinian woman who inspired my historical fiction novel, *Ester's Child*, soon to be released as an updated e-book.

Even after Lebanon, there was much to come. Several years later, I was to spend time in Israel, both on the western Jewish side and on the eastern Arab side. There were many nail-biting moments as I traveled from the Jewish sector to the Arab section. Tensions arose from every quarter. While visiting western Jerusalem, my sweetheart Jack and I were verbally attacked and threatened by conservative Jews. After traveling to the eastern Arab side, small children threw stones at our Arab driver's cab, compelling us to hastily flee the area. The land of Jewish Israel and of Arab Palestine grew only increasingly more dangerous.

When Iraq invaded Kuwait in August, 1990, I happened to be in the United States. I quickly arranged travel from Atlanta to London, Egypt, and Saudi Arabia where I interviewed fleeing Kuwaitis. I was invited to visit the city of Taif, where the Kuwaiti government-in-exile was established. There I was granted an interview with the emir as well as the crown prince. Thankfully, I was able to obtain the cooperation of the Kuwaiti government and the Kuwaiti people so that I was privy to their first-hand accounts of war and death. Those interviews and experiences became the number two *New York Times* bestseller, *The Rape of Kuwait.*

I also met Kuwait's wealthiest princess, the well-respected Souad al Sabah, wife of the only remaining son of Kuwait's longest-reigning emir, Mubarak the Great. I found Princess Souad to be a beautiful and fascinating woman, a highly regarded Arab poet, a mother devoted to her children, and a woman who was previously a great supporter of Saddam Hussein. She even wrote poems flattering Saddam, calling him the hope of the Arab people. Her palace was one of the few al-Sabah palaces not torched by Saddam's men, which triggered many hurtful Kuwaiti rumors over the reason her palatial home was spared.

Shortly after Iraq was expelled from Kuwait, I was invited to travel to Kuwait City on the Kuwaiti government sponsored "Freedom Flight." While in Kuwait I met with returning royals, including the Kuwaiti crown prince whom I had previously interviewed. The country was considered so volatile that the Kuwaiti ambassador to the United States and his invited guests planned for only a one-day visit. However, I slipped away from the party, did not re-board the plane, and remained in Kuwait for a month.

That month was one of the most exciting of my life. During my stay in Kuwait I lived through endless thrilling moments, including celebrations with Kuwaiti freedom fighters, a visit to the tent cities in which thousands of people were stranded between Iraq and Kuwait, and my entry into Iraq, an act forbidden by the American military. My visit to the "Highway of Death" with my volunteer driver, a young banker by profession named Saud A. al-Mutawa, shocked my senses. I waited with Kuwaiti mothers and fathers when the buses filled with Kuwaiti prisoners from Iraq were returned to Kuwait City. I was the only writer invited by the Kuwaiti government to meet with the women housed in a specially designated government building, all of whom had been brutally raped and impregnated by Iraqi soldiers. Most of the women were pleading for abortions, but the Kuwaiti government disappointed them by saying no.

In the spring of 1998, after reading that Saddam Hussein was no longer allowing American journalists or aid workers to enter Iraq, I wrote a letter to him requesting that he make an exception to grant me a visit visa. (I knew that no government official would have the courage or audacity to grant the author of *The Rape of Kuwait* permission and a visa to enter the country. I realized that I would have to go to the man who ruled all of Iraq, Saddam Hussein. I did, and my plan worked.) To my joyful surprise, I received a telephone call from

115

Saddam Hussein's offices in Baghdad saying that I was welcome to visit Iraq.

After traveling to New York to meet with the Iraqi officials attached to the United Nations, I was quickly provided with a visa and a letter stating that I should be given every courtesy. Since the U.S. led embargo did not allow flights into Iraq, I traveled to Amman, Jordan, rented a car and hired a Jordanian driver. I traveled twelve hours across the desert and went into Iraq alone, without knowing anyone. I spent the next three weeks visiting hospitals, women's organizations, and private homes.

My life was changed forever by that trip. One sweet benefit was that I met a woman who would become one of my dearest friends, a woman the world now knows as Mayada al-Askari, featured in the book, *Mayada, Daughter of Iraq.*

Other compelling sagas were in my future. I had the sad privilege of hearing first-hand the cruelties Saddam's regime inflicted upon the Kurdish people. This came after meeting Ra'ad al-Askari who introduced me to his baby sister, Joanna, who had lived through the deadly and ghastly chemical attacks upon an entire people. Joanna's story was told to the world in the book *Love in a Torn Land: One Woman's Daring Escape from Saddam's Poison Gas Attacks on the Kurdish People of Iraq.*

Yet another intriguing adventure unfolded when I came to know Omar and Zaina bin Laden, as well as Omar's mother, Najwa Bin Laden. Their stories are shared in the book *Growing Up Bin Laden*, the only book that reveals personal stories about Osama and his family.

After hearing the terror tales of the Taliban and of their dedicated assault upon the women of Afghanistan, I was eager to explore the true life story of an Afghan woman. That story arrived in the form of an amazing Afghan woman named Maryam Khail. Maryam is one of the boldest women one could meet, and her brave spirit is amazing to behold, told in the book *For the Love of a Son, One Afghan Woman's Quest for Her Stolen Child.*

Now looking back upon my life, I feel a strong desire to share the stories of the fascinating people I have known, and the exhilarating journeys I have lived. At this moment the excitement is building at the thought of reliving those days of anticipation and drama.

In *American Chick in Saudi Arabia*, I have given you a little taste of the beginning of my life of adventure. There is much more to come and I'm hoping that you get to share many other adventures with me.

Stay tuned!

Jean Sasson

For additional information about Jean Sasson and her books, including maps, timelines, glossaries, and key facts about Saudi Arabia, please visit the author's website: http://www.JeanSasson.com

Blog: http://jeansasson.wordpress.com/

Facebook: http://www.facebook.com/AuthorJeanSasson

Twitter: http://twitter.com/jeansasson

FOR THE LOVE
OF A SON

One Afghan woman's quest
for her stolen child

"Anyone with the slightest interest in human rights will
find this book heart-wrenching." -Betty Mahmoody,
author of *Not Without My Daughter*

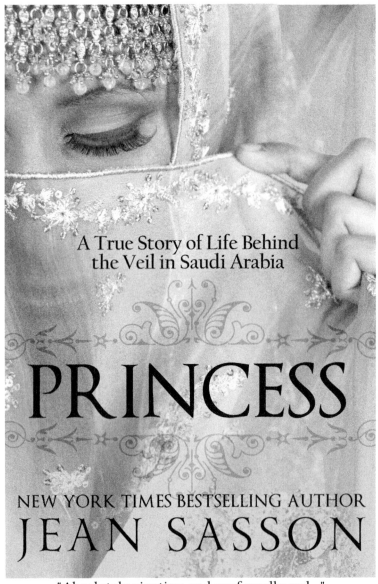

A True Story of Life Behind
the Veil in Saudi Arabia

PRINCESS

NEW YORK TIMES BESTSELLING AUTHOR
JEAN SASSON

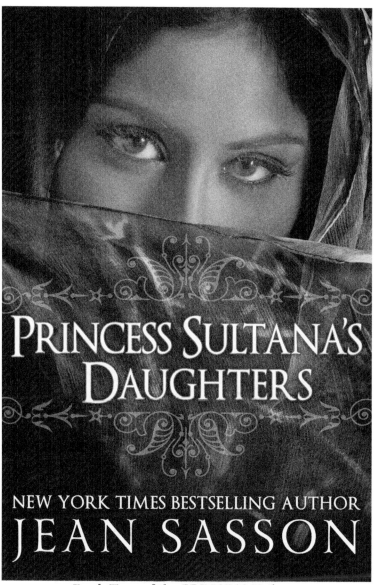

PRINCESS SULTANA'S DAUGHTERS

NEW YORK TIMES BESTSELLING AUTHOR

JEAN SASSON

Book Two of the PRINCESS Trilogy

Praise for PRINCESS: "A chilling story...a vivid account of an air-conditioned nightmare..." --*Entertainment Weekly*

PRINCESS SULTANA'S CIRCLE

NEW YORK TIMES BESTSELLING AUTHOR

JEAN SASSON

Book Three of the PRINCESS trilogy

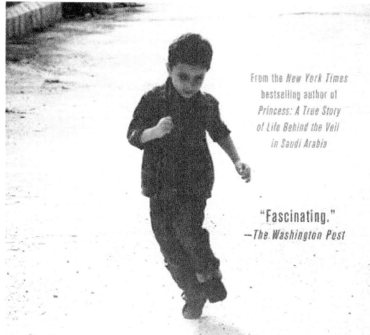

From the *New York Times*
bestselling author of
*Princess: A True Story
of Life Behind the Veil
in Saudi Arabia*

"Fascinating."
—*The Washington Post*

GROWING UP
BIN LADEN

OSAMA'S WIFE AND SON TAKE US
INSIDE THEIR SECRET WORLD

Najwa bin Laden | Omar bin Laden | Jean Sasson

"The most vivid look the American public has had at Bin
Laden's family life...The most complete account available."
--*New York Times*

"Fascinating." --*The Washington Post*

Printed in Great Britain
by Amazon

80814944R00071